God Bless!

Bad Roots: Bad Fruits

A Biblical Challenge to AHA/Abolish Human Abortion

Scott J Mahurin

Scott J Mahurin

For Bob George (1956-2017)

A faithful sidewalk counselor and friend

One must make sure when fighting with monsters that he does not become one himself.
-Frederick Nietzsche

Either make the tree good and its fruit good, or else make the tree bad and its fruit bad; for a tree is known by its fruit.
–Jesus Christ, speaking in Matthew 12:33

TABLE OF CONTENTS

Acknowledgments

Introduction: A Nation of Perverse Judgment

ACKNOWLEDGMENTS

Thank you to my lovely wife for her editing skills. I love you Rebecca.

Thank you to Joshua Steward for his illustration of the cover.

Thank you to Gulf Coast Community Church of St Petersburg, Florida for their faithful proclamation of the gospel.

Thank you to the Lord Jesus Christ for dying on the cross for my sins.

INTRODUCTION: A NATION OF PERVERSE JUDGMENT

O Lord, how long shall I cry,
And You will not hear?
Even cry out to You, "Violence!"
And You will not save.
Why do You show me iniquity,
And cause me to see trouble?
For plundering and violence are before me;
There is strife, and contention arises.
Therefore the law is powerless,
And justice never goes forth.
For the wicked surround the righteous;
Therefore perverse judgment proceeds.

Habakkuk 1:2-5 **NKJV**

3000 people will die today in the United States.

Not in a terrorist attack.

Not of a terminal illness.

Not of natural causes.

They will be ripped apart, decapitated, and shredded into

little pieces by "doctors" who legally perform surgical abortions.

Since 1973, over 60 million babies have been legally slaughtered in our land. 1/5 of our current total population has been lost forever. Approximately 1,000,000 babies per year are gone. If one saw these statistics out of context, they might assume these atrocities took place in an evil country completely devoid of biblical truth or influence. They might believe that this pagan nation had never heard the good news of Jesus Christ. But this is not the case. For the United States of America retains much of her Christian heritage. The atrocity of abortion continues despite the large numbers of Christians and their influence in society. Millions of evangelical Christians claim to be born again and say they believe the Bible is God's infallible word. Churches are still ubiquitous. But despite these horrific abortion numbers, few believe that abortion is America's greatest sin.

Look again at the numbers. Sixty million equals roughly the combined populations of Florida and California. If all the aborted babies in the United States since *Roe v Wade* populated their own country, this land of the slaughtered would rank as the 23rd most populated country in the world between France's 64 million and Italy's 59 million. Put simply, these are stupefying numbers. But despite this, many American Christians do not believe abortion is our greatest sin.

No terrorist or foreign dictator could ever accomplish what we have allowed by judicial fiat. It would take **ISIS** centuries to *come close* to what we have done to our own children. Even the Nazis would have taken at least a generation to reach these terrifying numbers in their concentration camps. But here in America, filled with her churches, Christians, Bibles and Christian schools, we remain a nation of perverse judgment, sitting under the wrath of God just as Habakkuk spoke of all those centuries ago.

God is good. Still, we know God sees all things. He is just.

We know, as Thomas Jefferson shuddered to note, that His justice will not sleep forever. So when we look at what we have allowed since 1973, we must realize every day we are given here in the United States is nothing more than an act of divine mercy. His mercy really does endure. How do we know this? He has not destroyed us for our wickedness for allowing and promoting this evil.

Isa. 5:20 tells us, "Woe to those who call evil good, and good evil; Who put darkness for light, and light for darkness; Who put bitter for sweet, and sweet for bitter!"

In our land, the vileness of murder is retold as "choice" or "reproductive rights."

However, during the 40 plus years of legal abortion since *Roe v Wade*, there have been encouraging moments for the pro-life movement. For example, one can look back on the "Summer of Mercy" in 1990 in Wichita, KS and the daring rescues of

Operation Rescue and Missionaries to the Preborn. The nationwide peaceful prayer vigil named 40 Days for Life has been an effective tool for closing clinics. Over 90 clinics have closed down from 2008-2018—due to the consistent prayerful presence of God's people.

And, not only are clinics closing down, but there has been a resurgence of pro-life ministry and activism in the United States. Young people in America are increasingly pro-life. A recent Boston Globe article states,

"Young Americans — <u>voters under 30</u> — were once the most gung-ho in support of unfettered legal abortion. In 1991, fully 36 percent believed abortion should be legal under any circumstances. But by 2010, 18-to-29-year-olds had become more pro-life than their parents — only 24 percent still wanted to keep abortion legal in all cases. More than any other age cohort, in fact, young adults are now the most likely to think abortion should be *illegal* in all circumstances." [1]

Also, Presidential candidates Mike Huckabee and Marco Rubio argued for a complete abortion ban during the Republican primaries of 2016–they were the first major Presidential candidates to do so. Gov. Huckabee and Sen. Rubio rightly exposed the flimsy legal foundation of the Supreme Court's fateful decision in 1973 from the largest political stage in the nation.

Additionally, we are seeing progress on the state and local political fronts as well. Personhood amendments have begun appearing on state and local ballots to protect all human life from the moment of conception to the point of natural death. The personhood amendments demonstrate a strong legal challenge to Roe vs. Wade. Why?

---

[1] Jacoby, Jeff. "American Millennials Rethink Abortion, for Good Reasons - The Boston Globe." *BostonGlobe.com,* 9 June 2015.

Supreme Court Justice Harry Blackmun, the author of the majority opinion of Roe vs. Wade decision in 1973, commented, "If this suggestion of personhood is established, the appellant's case, of course, collapses, for the fetus' right to life would then be guaranteed specifically by the Amendment." [2]

Modern technology is also on the side of life. Every year we see more and more visual technological advances. As this continues, so does the reinforcement that life begins at conception. Ultrasounds leave no doubt about the humanity of the preborn. It is now common for "gender reveals" and for expectant mothers and fathers, Christian and non-Christian alike, to name their preborn child before birth and reveal the name on social media.

Yes, there is good news on the horizon. As of September 2018, only 494 abortion clinics remain in the United States. In 1990, there were over 2,100. We observe only one out of every

[2] [2](Roden, Gregory J. Issues in Law & Medicine. 2010 Spring; 25(3): 185-273)
[3] http://abortiondocs.org/

four clinics remain open since 1990.[3]

But perhaps the most encouraging pro-life news broke in the summer of 2015, when the Center for Bio Medical Ethics exposed the sale of baby body parts at Planned Parenthood. And while David Daleiden of CMP was arrested for breaking the law in Texas, he was later acquitted, and all charges were dropped. It was true all along. Planned Parenthood was selling baby body parts, in violation of federal law. [4]

While their motivations, denominations, or theology may vary, any pro-life Christian can see all of this as a blessing and should echo a hearty *amen.* Yet even with this progress there have also been setbacks.

Since 1989, several abortion doctors were murdered on site at their respective clinics, prompting Congress to pass the 1994 Freedom of Access to Clinic Entrances Act (FACE). FACE passed the Senate and House with bi-partisan support. President

---

[4] Ertelt, Steven. "David Daledein Vindicated as Judge Dismissed Charges Against Him For Exposing Planned Parenthood." LifeNews.com, 16 June 2016.)

Bill Clinton then signed the bill into law. Only 30 Senators voted against it, including several who campaigned on the pro-life label. Sidewalk counselors and pro-life activists ministering at local abortion clinics have since been completely relegated to the sidewalks for fear of a 10-year minimum prison sentence.

More recently, the SCOTUS struck down a Texas law in 2016 requiring that abortion doctors have admitting privileges at local hospitals within a 30-mile radius and requiring that clinics have certain guidelines for medical emergencies. [5] That same year, a federal judge in Florida struck down similar legislation passed overwhelmingly by the Florida State House and Senate and signed by the Governor. [6]

There is undeniable tension between conservative states and the federal judiciary on the issue of abortion, and it does not seem to be going away anytime soon. Some constitutionalists, like

[5] (Liptak, Adam. "Supreme Court Strikes Down Texas Abortion Restrictions." *The New York Times,* 27 June 2016.)
[6] (Rohrer, Gary. "Federal Judge Blocks New Florida Abortion Law." *OrlandoSentinel.com,* 1 July 2016.)

Pastor Matt Trewhella, have researched and rediscovered the doctrine of the lesser magistrate which asserts the right of lower courts and magistrates to nullify the decisions of higher courts.

The battle lines are drawn. The pro-abortion arguments are becoming more and more strident. The political left is attempting to remove the shame and stigma of abortion. In doing so, they admit that such stigma exists, and show the law of God written on their consciences (Rom. 2). Sidewalk counselors, including myself, have been bullied online and in-person and threatened with lawsuits.

In 2013, I discovered that the radical pro-abortion group Voice of Choice had listed all of my personal information online. Since I am the Director of a pro-life, 501c3 publicly incorporated sidewalk counseling ministry, my information is pretty easily found. They posted my information and encouraged all comers to call, write, text, or email me to stop "bullying women so hatefully." Eventually pro-life groups filed a lawsuit, and Voice of Choice was forced to drop all pro-lifers' personal information contained on the site.[7]

A side note: I received only one text from a Boston area code telling me "to stop bullying with so much hate." Many pro-choicers are apparently tone deaf to irony.

Out of this environment, a group is emerging claiming to be abolitionists of abortion.

They proclaim themselves abolitionists in the spirit of the anti-slavery abolitionists William Lloyd Garrison and William Wilberforce. They wear self-styled abolitionist t-shirts and carry graphic signs. They have an impressive web presence on Facebook and other social media sites. They are Abolish Human Abortion, or AHA.

But are they really abolitionists or unbalanced church

---

[7] Yonke, Matt. "Voice of Choice Website Removes "Bully List" Targeting Pro-Life Activists With Harassment." LifeNews.com, 24 Oct. 2014, www.life.news.com/2014/10/23/voice-of-choice-website-removes-bully-list-targeting-pro-life-activists-with-harassment

haters?

Are they prophets of God or are they instruments of

destruction?

Are more Christians coming out to minister at the clinics

because of AHA or is the body of Christ actually turned away

from clinic ministry because of their toxicity?

It is for these and other questions that I wrote this small

booklet. We will examine the roots of AHA, and the fruit it is

currently bringing forth.

CHAPTER 1: GETTING ACQUAINTED

I was born in 1976, in Clarkston, a small town in Eastern Washington. I grew up across the Snake River in Lewiston, Idaho. As a boy, I had some exposure to the Christian faith, but did not come a came to a saving faith in Jesus until December 1992. While studying the Bible, I learned from Psalm 119 and Jeremiah 1 that abortion as murder and God is the author of all life. My pastors were very solid and principled on the abortion issue.

However, abortion was always on the backburner for many years. My hometown was at least 100 miles from the nearest abortion facility in Spokane. Even in high school I always considered myself pro-life. To me, this meant voting for the pro-life candidate and discouraging the practice of abortion.

Fast forward to 1999. My senior year at the University of Idaho, a group called the Center for Bio-Ethical Reform (CBR) visited the campus and brought with them graphic images of

abortion. They displayed them on campus for several days and

used this as an educational and evangelistic tool with the students

and professors of the UI. One of their missionaries stayed with

my roommate and me for a couple days. I was amazed that there

was a such a thing as a "pro-life" missionary. I was intrigued.

This was the first time I had ever "seen" an abortion. The

graphic images haunt me to this day. I can vividly remember

standing in front of the library the first time I ever saw a picture of

an aborted baby.

But, as it so often does, life went on. I got married, started

a family, worked, paid bills, and got older. Abortion remained in

the periphery. Somewhere between college and my 30s we

moved across the country to Florida. So it wasn't until 2007 when

the LORD awakened me to more pro-life activism. My pastor,

Jerry Cisar, preached a sermon on Mother's Day that would

change my life. He preached about abortion. He was not preaching about any specific type of activism, but it was a general call to become aware. To wake up. It worked. The sermon title was, "The Number One Problem in America Today." The LORD used it greatly to move abortion to the front of my mind and to produce conviction in my heart.

After this sermon, I did some research. I found that abortion was everywhere in Florida. I learned there were even *five abortion clinics* in St Petersburg. Many *states* don't even have five clinics. I began to go to the clinics, and there I met other pro-life Christians doing this thing called "sidewalk counseling." Despite having lived in St Petersburg for three years, I was unaware of the abortion holocaust existing down the street from me. I was asleep. I was apathetic. But the LORD woke me up. I began to research the various clinics and started going to the sidewalk with others while still teaching and tutoring full-time.

In 2011, I went to Mississippi to learn some sidewalk counseling methods from Cal Zastrow and Personhood USA. I talked to my pastors and elders. I got advice. I prayed. The next year, in September 2012, I officially launched Florida Preborn Rescue. I wanted to connect pro-life belief with pro-life action. Florida has almost 20,000,000 residents. Millions of Floridians consider themselves to be pro-life. Over four million attend conservative pro-life churches. But very few are actually involved in a sidewalk counseling ministry.

My goal in launching FPR was simple. To end abortion in Florida through peaceful and prayerful sidewalk counseling by the mobilization of local churches on-site at local abortion clinics.

I didn't realize it at the time, but a group called Abolish Human Abortion was getting started too. At first, I was glad to see people who appeared to be like minded co-laborers. Anyone involved in on-site activism at abortion clinics knows it is difficult and often lonely. It can be very discouraging to see other

ministries filled and overflowing while pro-life ministries (if any)

barely hang on. It can be challenging to find volunteers and more

challenging still to constantly explain sidewalk counseling to our

brothers and sisters in Christ.

I was happy to see a group so vocal and seemingly

uncompromising on the internet. I began following some of the

AHA groups on Facebook to network with them. I liked what I

saw and considered myself a kindred spirit to their efforts. I

shared some of their pictures on my social sites and began

sending them my newsletters.

And then I met my first representative of Abolish Human
Abortion.

Part of my ministry duties include teaching Christ-

centered sidewalk counseling principles and methods in St

Petersburg and Tampa. I have done this now since 2013 and

have taught over 100 Christians the basic "do's and don'ts" of sidewalk counseling. These classes have equipped many to come to the sidewalk and minister in our city.

One Saturday afternoon, I was teaching a class at a local coffee shop. The class had several attendees and the discussion was very informal. A middle-aged lady showed up about ten minutes after the class began. I welcomed her and offered her some coffee. She declined. She seemed distracted and bothered from the beginning. She began interrupting me and eventually took over the discussion. This was a new experience for me. I decided to just go with it.

Looking back, I was so shocked that I did not know what to do. She started rebuking me for not doing enough to end abortion. I told her politely I had been at the abortion clinic on Central Avenue in St Petersburg every Saturday except for illness and my recent wedding and honeymoon for the past six years. I had no idea what she was talking about. It turns out she was angry at me because the school where I was teaching (I am not sure how she found out this information, though in the Age of Zuckerberg how hard can it be?) met in a church near an abortion clinic. She assumed that since a) I had not spoken to the pastor of the church about the abortion issue and b) since the abortion clinic near the school is still open, it was all my fault. So she began to rebuke me in the name of Jesus. You never have your copy of "How to Win Friends and Influence People" when you need it, do you?

Anyway, she did not listen, she just kept on talking. She began calling me to repent. She said I was compromised. Now, I know I am not perfect. Only Jesus is. But this was a strange meeting. Easily the weirdest class I had ever taught!

I tried asking her questions about her background, and how she got involved in pro-life ministry. The few answers she gave were very telling.

She told me she was not "pro-life" but that she was an "abolitionist." She took great offense at the term "pro-life." It was as though I called her a Planned Parenthood supporter or a Yankees fan or something. I had never heard this distinction before, but this distinction was *very* important to her. I tried to get some sense of the definition she was using, but all I could gather was that she was more pro-life than me because she was an "abolitionist." She goes to meetings (like mine, apparently) and churches and asks Christians what they are doing about child sacrifice. Even pro-life missionaries aren't doing enough. It seemed odd that she would pick me, since I am the director of a pro-life ministry in St Petersburg.

Every Christian has their areas of service. My area is pro-life ministry and sidewalk counseling. I could count maybe four or five other people who have been as active on the sidewalk in Tampa Bay since I began Florida Preborn Rescue. Please hear me out. This is not being braggadocious, I am just retelling the story. Finally, it hit me.

She was attacking me for *not being an abolitionist.*

Now, I am going to tell you something about myself. You don't even need to confirm with my wife, my children, my parents, my siblings, my in-laws, or even my brothers and sisters at my church. I am a sinner. I immediately thought of the old story in 2 Samuel 20 of David and Shimei. Maybe, I deserved the rebuke from this lady. But her theology would soon expose her confusion.

After asking her questions about her church, she told me that she had no church or elders but that she was part of the "universal church." She was part of the "bride of Christ." According to her, churches are compromised on the issue of abortion. So she was going around to churches on Sundays and protesting them, since she was not attending a church of her own.

Interesting.

This was my introduction to the group Abolish Human Abortion.

While every group has its respective nutjobs, I quickly found her personality and rhetoric to be sadly indicative of AHA the more I interacted with them.

In 2016, Abolish Human Abortion began circulating a petition to the Florida House of Representatives criminalizing abortion and making abortion a felony for anyone *procuring or performing* an abortion. I was approached on the sidewalk on a Saturday by some AHA members and asked if I would sign it. Since it has always been my goal to work with different pro-life groups as much as I can, I happily agreed. However, after I signed the petition, I began to have second thoughts. After further reflection, and rereading it, I believed that there was a loophole in the petition that would potentially leave women vulnerable to prosecution for having an abortion, which has never been done in the history of the United States, even when abortion was illegal.

A few days later, I received an email from a self-proclaimed "abolitionist" asking if AHA could post the petition on my Facebook page. When I politely told this "abolitionist" that I had questions about the wording of the Amendment, and I would be happy to distribute a different petition with different wording, the young man (he was all of 20 years old) began to rebuke me for "hindering the work of abolition" and not understanding the significance of God's law.

It is not difficult to be taken aback by the arrogance and bombast of this statement. This is certainly not a good way to win allies, but allies are not needed apparently when you are so convinced that your way alone is right. AHA representatives are convinced they are the only uncompromised Christians currently working to make abortion illegal. If Abolish Human Abortion desires to sponsor bills and legislation that would immediately outlaw abortion, this is a noble goal.

But total abortion bans are failing to pass. During the spring of 2016, a member of the Florida House of Representatives, Charles Van Zant, sponsored a total abortion ban (House Bill 203). While noble, the bill couldn't even get out of committee despite an overwhelming Republican majority and a Republican governor. HB 203 couldn't get out of committee to a full vote in a conservative state. My point is simple. The reality of political scheming and cowardice will keep any significant abortion ban at bay for some time.

Abolish Human Abortion sponsoring total abortion bans is fine. But taking the next step to prosecuting women who have had abortions is not just immoral, but completely foolhardy given our current political situation. Rhetorically decapitating those who disagree with you is not helpful, especially if you are slapping around your brothers and sisters in Christ.

Without a doubt, sincere Christians are involved in AHA. My hope is that this small booklet will encourage all of them to search the Scriptures and grow in the LORD. As I have studied Abolish Human Abortion, I have learned their zeal is great. But zeal without temperament is dangerous. AHA needs to repent and reform themselves according to the Scriptures just like every other pro-life group. I pray that they join local churches. I pray that they encourage church leaders and repent of their slander against the church. I pray that they can learn to work with others, like their heroes William Lloyd Garrison and William Wilberforce, whom they so rightly admire.

Every Christian in the United States, if they are involved at all in the pro-life movement, has had to learn as they go. Let us learn the wisdom of Phil. 3:16 and "live up to what we have already attained." As Pastor Jon Speed has said, "none of us are born with the AHA symbol tattooed on our bodies." The members of Abolish Human Abortion are no more pro-life than anyone else in the movement. We all have had to come to the knowledge of Christ. We all have had to come to the realization that babies are being murdered in our culture. Some Christians live hundreds of miles away from their nearest abortion facility. Some are involved in various pro-life ministries listed earlier. And all of us are wrestling with the most biblical and God honoring way to speak up for the voiceless.

If the zeal of AHA can be tempered with some biblical knowledge, if they can mature in biblical and spiritual understanding, repent of their self-appointed prophet complex, understand sound ecclesiology, and submit to local church leadership, Abolish Human Abortion can be reformed and made useful. But this will require significant change. They must come to a biblical understanding of the church and her offices. They must come to a biblical understanding of grace and mercy. They must humble themselves and join hands with others striving to end abortion in America. Otherwise the work of saving babies will be hindered.

The bad roots of AHA are found in individualism, self-righteousness and hostility to the bride of Christ. The bad fruits are obvious in the divisions they cause. Many churches are completely turned off by their approach. This causes problems for those of us who are also seeking to do full-time pro-life ministry alongside local churches.

AHA needs to repent.

May God grant them repentance and use them for His glory.

CHAPTER TWO: What is AHA?

"...bringing the gospel into conflict with the evil of our age,

following in the footsteps of the former abolitionist movements,

we aim to end one of the greatest miseries and moral evils ever to

be entrenched in our world. Human beings are created in the

image of Almighty God, the very Creator of the Universe. The

weakest and most helpless among us have been subjected by this

wicked culture to accepted, legal, and systematic destruction. We

are simply attempting to answer the question: What does

Christianity look like in a culture that practices child sacrifice?"

And put our answer into action." [8]

I can say amen to much of the above statement. Babies

are being destroyed every day. We *need* to end abortion. And

Christians *should be* on the frontlines. Yes. So far, so good. I'm

there. Too many churches and Christians are silent on this issue,

---

[8] *www.abolishhumanabortion.com*

or their activism is reduced to voting every four years for the most pro-life candidate. More definitely needs to be done. Amen. But their last sentence is where we differ.

Toby Harmon and T. Russell Hunter are several of the "founders" of Abolish Human Abortion. They are not mentioned by name on the website. Both men live in the Norman, OK area. They are in their late 30s or early 40s. They are nice-looking, bearded men who carry graphic signs and design t-shirts. I have had some brief contact with them and they are very polite and genuine. I trust their motives are good. They have an impressive web presence. As of this writing, there are hundreds of videos on YouTube that either Hunter or Harmon or other AHA acolytes have produced. Hunter is a gifted artist and graphic designer.

Abortion has been legal longer than Harmon, Hunter and I have been alive. For the record, I turned 42 in November 2018.

So, none of us have been battling abortion for our whole lives. Legal abortion is older than we are. As a result, we can learn from those pro-life groups in existence since abortion became legal. It's odd, really. They wholeheartedly reject the label pro-life and call themselves abolitionists.

AHA loves the history of abolitionism but fails to acknowledge the history of the pro-life movement. But we must learn the history of the pro-life movement. Both Protestants and Catholics have worked together for the common good. They have all been working longer than Hunter, Harmon and myself have been alive. In fact, my Catholic friend Ethel has been praying at the same abortion clinic in St Petersburg since 1975.

However, the rub comes in with the answer to their own question. For when they say, "What does Christianity look like in a culture that practices child sacrifice?" they ignore that other pro-life groups are answering that same question, and some of them in very different ways.

Let's analyze the statements above. Some of the roots are mentioned here. Let's examine the fruit.

AHA is "Bringing the gospel into conflict with the evil of our age."

Right. But the gospel is *already* in conflict with the evil of our age. Light always conflicts with darkness. Wicked Cain hated righteous Abel. The seed of the woman will always be in conflict with the seed of the serpent (Gen. 3:15) until Jesus returns. It is unnecessary to *bring the gospel into conflict* when it is already in conflict by its *very nature.*

The Apostle John says, "The Light shines in the darkness, and the darkness did not comprehend it," and "this is the condemnation, that the light has come into the world, and men loved darkness rather than light, because their deeds were evil" (Jn. 1:5, 3:19). Conflict is inescapable.

The Apostle Paul tells us that the "carnal mind cannot understand the things of God (Rom. 8:6-8), and "the carnal mind is opposed to the spiritual" (1 Cor 2:14). There is no neutral ground between the unbelieving mind and the Christian mind. These are basic Christian doctrines. We must understand this.

Paul was "provoked" in Acts 17 because he saw the city of Athens given over to idols. But his tone at Mars Hill was warm and polite, even to the atheists and wicked idolaters of Athens. While Paul did experience conflict because of the gospel, he dealt with it in a specific way. Let's look at Acts 17:22-34.

"Then Paul stood amid the Areopagus and said, "Men of Athens, I perceive that in all things you are very religious; [23] for as I was passing through and considering the objects of your worship, I even found an altar with this inscription: TO THE UNKNOWN GOD. Therefore, the One whom you worship without knowing, Him I proclaim to you: [24] "God, who made the world and everything in it, since He is Lord of heaven and earth, does not dwell in temples made with hands.[25] Nor is He worshiped with men's hands, as though He needed anything, since He gives to all life, breath, and all things. [26] And He has made from one blood[c] every nation of men to dwell on all the face of the earth, and has determined their preappointed times and the boundaries of their dwellings, [27] so that they should seek the Lord, in the hope that they might grope for Him and find Him, though He is not far from each one of us; [28] for in Him we live and move and have our being, as also some of your own poets have said, 'For we are also His offspring.' [29] Therefore, since

we are the offspring of God, we ought not to think that the Divine Nature is like gold or silver or stone, something shaped by art and man's devising. [30] Truly, these times of ignorance God overlooked, but now commands all men everywhere to repent, [31] because He has appointed a day on which He will judge the world in righteousness by the Man whom He has ordained. He has given assurance of this to all by raising Him from the dead." [32] And when they heard of the resurrection of the dead, some mocked, while others said, "We will hear you again on this *matter*." [33] So Paul departed from among them. [34] However, some men joined him and believed, among them Dionysius the Areopagite, a woman named Damaris, and others with them."

The above passage serves as a primer for public ministry. Paul did not compromise the truth of his message. However, you can almost feel the warmth coming from his words. He compliments them by being religious, even though they were pagan. He used persuasion and rhetoric. He proclaimed truth in a winsome way. You do not get the sense from this passage that he was derisive or angry, as evidenced by his invite back to the Areopagus. And we are told that some believed the message and joined him. *He was provoked in his spirit, but he wasn't unhinged in his words.*

So, let's go back to AHA's original question.

"So, what does Christianity look like in a culture that practiced child sacrifice?"

Is AHA the only group allowed to answer this question?

And do they think they are the first group to do so?

Crisis pregnancy centers answer this question.

Sidewalk counselors answer this question.

Pro-life political action committees answer this question.

Because adoption agencies answer this question.

Large families who have lots of children answer this question.

Christianity looks like all of the above.

For abortion to be illegal and unthinkable in the United States, we need EVERYONE to participate. There are lots of ways to end abortion and praise Jesus, lots of groups that seek to end it. We need pregnancy centers, abstinence education, strong pastors and strong families, sidewalk counselors who are funded by the local church, and strong pro-life lawmakers and judges. We need everybody!

Every movement of social change has needed large numbers of diverse foot soldiers. Does AHA really think the Civil Rights movement would have happened without Protestants and Catholics, conservatives and liberals, and blacks and whites working together for the common cause?

It doesn't take long when interacting with anyone from Abolish Human Abortion to notice something. They thrive on conflict. They specialize and even brag about "agitating" others into becoming an audience for their claims. Many of the online videos have AHA representatives holding up signs in front of local churches. People are disturbed by the graphic signs and come over to ask them to stop showing them or take them down. Of course, the AHA crew does not. If elders or deacons come out to talk to the protestors, then these church leaders are asked a series of questions about "what they are doing to prevent the abortion holocaust." Obviously, these are loaded questions that do not want an honest answer, they are merely questions meant to produce a result. The result is a new heroic video starring AHA agitators and compromised pastors. Again, we see some of the roots mentioned earlier and the corresponding fruit produced.

Many in the pro-life movement are similar to adherents of Abolish Human Abortion, who believe they do not represent God or the Bible well unless people mad at them. Some of this is understandable. Many Christians are embarrassed of God's word, and many refuse to speak hard truths to the culture at large. This is part of the mess we are in.

But of course, the Bible tells us how to shine the light in the darkness, how to help our brothers and sisters overcome their fears. We are called to be loving of our brothers and sisters and to be peaceable and "*willing to yield*" (James 3:17). We are not to think of ourselves as *any better than anyone else* (Phil. 2). We are to avoid all *sectarianism* (Num 11:28, 1 Cor. 1:12-13).

Furthermore, nowhere in the New Testament are Christians called to agitate other Christians. We are not to have the same "roots" as Abolish Human Abortion. We must have the fruits of the Spirit.

AHA's favorite verse is Eph. 5:11, "Have nothing to do with the works of darkness, but rather expose them."

Oddly, if there was an argument to be made for this agitation, it can only take place in the context of a local church. This is a problem for acolytes of Abolish Human abortion because they deny the necessity of local churches. The book of Ephesians is a letter written to the *church at Ephesus.*

Abolish Human Abortion is rooted in agitation from the

anti-slavery abolitionists. They have not been tempered with the fellowship and fruits of the Spirit that are to be borne out in a local church setting. It is this and other inconsistencies that we will discuss in the next chapter.

CHAPTER THREE:
IDEOLOGY OR PRAGMATISM: A FALSE CHOICE

When looking at any organization or church or ministry, it is absolutely essential to carefully examine that group's theology. By theology, I mean simply this: What do they believe about God? What do they believe about man? What do they believe about sin? What do they believe about the church? What do they believe about the truth? What are the roots and foundation of your organization?

AHA has no official theology or statement of faith so we're not off to a good start. Adherents of Abolish Human Abortion reiterate that they are not a church. They aren't. This is true. They are not a church. Often, they claim they are not an organization, but an idea, or a movement, or an ideology. Confused? Join the club. Many conversations go like this.

Curious Chris: "Excuse me, sir. I think I saw you

protesting at a church last Sunday. Are you part of AHA?"

AHA Guy: "I can't be part of something that is an ideology or movement or symbol or an idea. These things cannot be part of anything. AHA is not a group."

Curious Chris: "Right, but don't you have an AHA shirt, an AHA hat, and aren't you holding an AHA sign?"

AHA Guy: "You need to repent."

Curious Chris: "Uh...."

You should be confused because this is very illogical. Abolish Human Abortion does have a "Declaration of Abolitionist Sentiments." Found on their website, it begins this way: "AHA is fully autonomous, ideologically driven, abolitionist societies coming together under Christ the King to speak with one voice."

According to the website, the Coalition "serves three important and limited purposes: to foster unity and cooperation among the various abolitionist societies that are a part of the

Abolish Human Abortion movement, to provide a platform for making statements and resolutions on behalf of the movement as a whole, and to define and protect the meaning of the Abolish Human Abortion symbol and the ideology it represents."[9]

Let's walk through these statements one at a time.

1. <u>AHA societies are fully autonomous.</u>

Now we are getting to some doctrine. But it's not very good doctrine. The word autonomous means "self-ruled." This sounds good on the surface, especially to American Protestants. We're all about self-rule, representative government, and reading the Bible for ourselves. However, there is a problem. You cannot be both fully-autonomous and all speak "with one voice." This is self-contradictory. This is illogical. You can't all be united if there is no accountability from the outside ensuring the mission of the organization goes forward. Strong organizations are accountable to others to direct and ensure the organization's success. And

---

[9] http://abolishhumanabortion.com/international-coalition-of-abolitionist-societies/

God's plan for accountability requires the local church (Hebrews

13; Matthew 18). Note the biblical inconsistencies with AHA.
Despite their intentions, Abolish Human Abortion's lack

of a formal structure causes concern. Are all voices equal in

AHA? Do the voices of Harmon and Hunter outweigh the

others? If not, why not? Who directs the activities of the group?

Who determines if there is sufficient unity and cooperation? If

there is not unity, is there a discipline structure in place? Who is

managing the finances of the AHA store?

There are no clear answers to these questions despite the

number of videos and productions produced by AHA. But since

nowhere on their impressive web presence are these questions

addressed, they are difficult to comprehend. Abolish Human

Abortion actually contributes to the confusion by not having

specific teaching or positions on these subjects. If an AHA

representative does something stupid or immoral, then the

leaders distance themselves, and say that this person is not really representative of their group. After all, they claim, "AHA is a symbol, not an organization." And according to AHA representatives, you can't be part of an ideology or movement or symbol or idea—they are not an organization. This illogical stance is actually a brilliant way to avoid accountability.

The most that we can gather is that Abolish Human Abortion sees themselves as the new Garrisons and Wilberforces but EVERYONE else is compromised.

2. Ideologically driven

Here are some common claims that AHA and its representatives often make.

"AHA is not an organization, it's a movement or ideology."

"AHA is not a group, it's an ideology."

 "AHA is not an organization, it's a movement."

"AHA doesn't do X, because AHA is a movement."

This is a real problem philosophically. It doesn't

take much rumination on the above statement to see its vacuity. This non-organization is incorporated and has financial statements. It has leaders despite their names not appearing online. You can "join" the "non-organization" by contacting "Directors of Abolitionist Societies around the country."

Abolish Human Abortion claims to be ideologically driven, and that's fine. The problem is that *everyone is ideologically driven.* Abolish Human Abortion is like the kid who is so excited he got a PS4 for Christmas. He thinks he's the only one, until he goes back to school and finds everyone else got one, too. Every group and every individual has a set of ideals that they *put into practice pragmatically.* For example, if you are hungry, you eat, and if you are thirsty, you pour yourself a nice beverage. The ideal of satisfying one's hunger and thirst is met by the pragmatic step of eating and drinking. This is not rocket science. Planned Parenthood is ideologically driven. The Republican Party is ideologically driven. McDonald's is ideologically driven.

And so is Abolish Human Abortion. But, by trumpeting their ideologically drivenness as a virtue opposed to pragmatism, AHA reveals their confusion between theological and practical terminology.

Pragmatism—or taking steps to reach a goal— is an enemy to Abolish Human Abortion. But everyone is a pragmatist. Even AHA has pragmatists. It only matters what ideals you are advancing pragmatically. The question is not *whether* you have ideals, but *which* ideals you advance. Everyone is ideological. It only matters which ideology you have. Everyone is pragmatic too, for everyone takes steps to achieve their ideological goals pragmatically. The question is simple. Is our ideology biblical or not?

Here is an example:

The Bible says that Christians should marry Christians and not be unequally yoked with non-Christians (1 Corinthians 7).

Once when I was in high school, a young lady asked me if I would ever date someone who didn't share my religious views. I told her, "No." When she asked me if I thought that was "like, discrimination?" I told her that "Yes, it was." The point is this. Christians are commanded to marry other Christians. That is the ideology. The pragmatism of this ideology is found when Christians pray for a godly spouse, go to church, become members, and realize (hopefully, soon) that more dateable and marriable Christians of the opposite sex are there and not on Tinder.

When Christians are part of singles' ministries, when they pray and seek the wisdom and counsel of others along the way, they understand the ideology found in 1 Corinthians 7. They follow the ideology by making practical steps pragmatically. There is no biblical inconsistency.

3. Abolitionist societies.

By societies, AHA means organizations (or, non

organizations?) many of which meet on Sunday instead of church in clear violation of Hebrews 13. Yet another biblical inconsistency.

Further, the Coalition exists to:

1. "Foster unity and cooperation among the various abolitionist societies that are a part of AHA."

2. "Provide a platform for making statements and resolutions on behalf of the movement."

3. "Define and protect the meaning of the AHA symbol and ideology it represents."

The roots of Abolish Human Abortion's Coalition of Abolitionist Societies are well-intentioned, but their fruits are confusing and misleading. Let's take a closer look at this discussion as to the purpose of the Coalition in the next chapter.

CHAPTER 4:

THE DECLARATION OF ABOLITIONIST SENTIMENTS

Clearly influenced by the anti-slavery abolitionists of antebellum America, the Declaration of Abolitionist Sentiments s stands as close to a "statement of faith" that we can find for the Abolish Human Abortion's Coalition of Abolitionist Societies.

The full declaration of sentiments is available on their website at www.abolishhumanabortion.com/international-coalition-of-abolitionist-societies.

Let's walk through some of these sentiments. I have chosen 31. Their quotes are in *italics*. My comments are below each number.

1. *"We are determined to live consistent Christian lives in the midst of a culture that kills its children and work to bring about the abolition of abortion."*

Without a church? If AHA wishes to accomplish this without the local church, they will be unsuccessful at best, and heretical at worst. We need the larger body of Christ. We need each other (1 Cor. 12; Heb. 10:24-25). This goes beyond "abolitionist fellowships" too, for the church at large would benefit from AHA's zeal and motivation. But when they isolate themselves, they seek and promote only their own agenda (Prov. 18:1).

2. *"The abolitionists denounced the constitutional compromise that permitted the institution of chattel slavery as "an agreement with Hell and a covenant with death."*

Right. Sort of. Recall that John Adams and other founding fathers were opposed to slavery. But they rightly believed that allowing the southern states to keep their slaves was an *incremental* step to eventually abolishing slavery completely. Remember that everyone is ideological and takes steps to achieve their ideological goals pragmatically. Adams and others knew that without this compromise, the Confederacy would have been an independent slaveholding nation. This "agreement with hell" helped end slavery.

3. *"The culture did not heed their call...as a result God judged their culture and brought war upon their nation. A bloody, war, and an unnecessary war."*

Actually, if they are talking about the Civil War, then it was definitely necessary.

Why? The war was necessary because abolitionism and its abolitionists failed. Here AHA participates in some breathtaking historical revisionism. Think about this for a second— Abolish Human Abortion talks about "laying the ax to the root of unbelief" and "ending child sacrifice." They rightly cite Wilberforce and Garrison as examples. Wilberforce led the fight to end the slave trade, but it took almost 20 years of legal squabbling in England. Garrison worked tirelessly in the United States. But if *the standard* is ending slavery, then both Wilberforce and Garrison are utter failures, because abolitionists did not end slavery. The Civil War did. The anti-slavery Amendments to the US Constitution did. In the United States, the war was necessary because the abolitionist movement, while noble, was ultimately failed. *Or you can view the abolitionists and the Civil War as a pragmatic step in the greater cause to end slavery.*

Now, one may argue that the abolitionists' agitation aided the process of speeding up the abolition of slavery, but only as a means for getting the south to secede more quickly. The presidential election of 1860 helped in this regard too. The southern states left the Union as soon as Abraham Lincoln was elected. War was imminent. The slaves would be freed several years later. But even if we grant this point to the AHA, we must grant it as *incrementalists.* The Civil War, abolitionist amendments, and the first shots at Fort Sumter were all incremental steps toward the ultimate goal of ending slavery. Nothing happened immediately.

4. *"But thanks be to God there remained a remnant of faithful followers who repented of their complacency, ceased to do*

evil, and learned to do good. A remnant that showed mercy,

sought to correct oppression and worked to establish justice."

What are they talking about? What remnant? The

abolitionist movement that failed, by their own definition of

success? This is illogical. The abolitionists were incrementalists

and pragmatists. While we're asking questions, how long did this

justice take to be administered? One could argue that the

injustices prevalent in the laws of the United States were not

overturned until the 1960s and the Civil Rights Act. Wilberforce

and Garrison had been dead for 130 and 84 years, respectively.

So, AHA abolitionists' examples, Wilberforce and Garrison

cannot be part of the remnant, for they were long gone from

putting their own answers into action.

5. *"But the cost was great, decades of unwilling repentance and*
   terrible violence forced reform disguised as Reconstruction,
   and the turmoil surrounding civil rights that remains with us
   to this day."

It took 100 years *after* the Civil War for the Civil Rights Act to be signed. It took 100 years of *incrementalist* legislation that led to the Civil Rights Act. In 1946, President Harry S Truman desegregated the Armed Forces. In 1947, Jackie Robinson broke the color barrier in Major League Baseball. In 1954, the Supreme Court ruled that segregated schools were unconstitutional, striking down the generations-old separate but equal clause of *Plessey v Ferguson*. In 1964, President Lyndon Johnson signed the Civil Rights Act. The following year he signed the Voting Rights Act. Several years later, the Fair Housing Act became law.

Jim Crow was dead. *Years of incremental legislation drove the stake through his heart.*

6. *"Any person who knowingly procures or performs an abortion is guilty of murder in the eyes of God and ought to be tried and found guilty of murder in a court of law. Any person who knowingly aids or abets a person in the*

procurement or performance of an abortion is guilty of being

an accessory to murder in a court of law."

How do you prove murder, which involves premediated malice, in the case of abortion? Certainly, some women know they are murdering their babies. But others are coerced. But some do so out of ignorance. While it is true that every abortion involves the premeditated killing of a human being, but not all abortions involve the same circumstances and knowledge by those involved. Besides, how does the punishment for the woman of an uninformed or coerced woman establish justice for the preborn?

Advocating for such a punishment is politically unrealistic and immoral. Yet another biblical inconsistency. Also, before *Roe v Wade,* when abortion was illegal in the United States, no state laws punished women for abortion.

7. *"We are a sinful nation. A people laden with iniquity. We have forsaken the Lord. The whole head is sick. The whole heart is faint. From the sole of the foot even to the head,*

there is no soundness in it, only wounds bruises, and

putrefying sores." (Isa. 1:5-6)

This is some flashy rhetoric. But it is not exactly true.

Apparently, everyone is sick—except AHA. In fact, one wonders

when they read this, if Abolish Human Abortion considers

themselves to be part of the sickness. Are they not covenantally

bound to what Isaiah laments? Or are they separated self-

righteously from our immoral land? The roots of AHA are

showing.

In Genesis 18, Abraham has a conversation with God. He

asks God how many righteous people it would take for Him to

relent of the upcoming destruction of Sodom and Gomorrah.

Abraham talked Him down, from forty to thirty, all the way to ten

men. God told Abraham, "For the sake of ten men, I will not

destroy it." Are there more than ten righteous left in the United

States? Probably. There are millions of Christians doing good

work in our country despite what AHA would have you believe.

We need to work together to end abortion. It is up to the LORD whether He wishes to grant our land mercy or not.

8. *"In the United States, for the past four decades, those who claim to be "pro-life" have relied primarily on politicians, para church ministries, and social justice organizations to get the job done."*

Maybe...or maybe not. Let's look at the scoreboard then, gang. The game is not over yet. However, the numbers don't lie. From an all-time high of 2176 in 1990, there are now 483 abortion clinics in the United States (as of September 2018) This is a decrease of 78%. Over the last 25 years, **1693** abortion clinics have closed in the United States. Closed forever. Babies are not being murdered in these clinics. Should every clinic be closed? Yes. But we aren't there yet. We should rejoice that so many clinics have been closed. This is good news. This is not bad news. This is progress. We need to keep going. [10] We keep taking

---

[10] (http://abortiondocs.org/closed-clinics/

incremental steps to pragmatically meet the ideological goal of ending abortion in America.

9. *"...the vast majority of Americans have chosen to take the other side of the road and have largely ignored their most innocent, oppressed, and endangered neighbors."*

Ok, is AHA talking about non-Christians or Christians? If non-Christians, are they expecting the nation of selfish idolaters and wicked oppressors to stand up for justice? This is not sensical. This is illogical. Yes, our nation has allowed this. By and large, we are a nation that has rejected God. A wicked culture that will never establish justice. Yet millions of faithful Christians here in America are working to end abortion.

10. *"Most people justify their apathy towards the ongoing genocide of preborn human beings with statements such as "All we can do is vote," "My church supports a local crisis pregnancy center," "My pastor preaches against abortion every year..."*

While AHA doesn't approve these incremental

actions, *actions* are not apathy. Actions are kind of the opposite

of apathy. Apathy literally means "without feeling" or "without

emotion." It is true that many American Christians merely use

the ballot box as a means of activism. Many churches also fund

pregnancy care centers that save babies every day. Some churches

are beginning to fund sidewalk counseling ministries too. And

there are pastors who preach against abortion. Those who vote

have actually made a difference. It is not all they can do, to be

sure. But it is something.

Even if we granted Abolish Human Abortion's

lament, incremental legislation saves lives. [11]

Dr. Michael New, Professor of Economics at Ave Maria

University, has researched the impact of "incremental legislation"

in the pro-life movement for several years. He is published in

~~many peer-reviewed and well~~-respected academic journals around

[11] (Hagelin, Rebecca. "New Study Shows Pro-Life Laws Save Lives." *The Heritage Foundation*,

www.heritage.org/marriage-and-family/commentary/new-study-shows-pro-life-laws-save-lives.)

the world. Dr. New has found three main arguments in favor of
incremental legislation:

1. "Incremental laws can inform people about the
   extreme nature of abortion policy in the United States
   and can shift public opinion in a more pro-life
   direction."

2. "A well-designed incremental law that gets challenged
   in court might eventually lead to the repeal of *Roe v
   Wade.*"

3. "Lives ARE saved." [12]

11. *"...every year the pro-life people of America await the next
    election to vote for a president who might get the
    opportunity to appoint judges who could shift the balance of
    the Supreme Court who might then be able to overturn Roe
    vs. Wade. And every year is like the previous forty-two,
    wherein more than a million of our smallest, most innocent,*

[12] Hays, Steve, et al. Abolition of Reason: Pro-Life Apologists Deconstruct
"Immediatist" Ideology as Presented in Cunningham-Hunter Debate.
JillStanek.com, 2015, www.jillstanek.com/wp/wp-
content/uploads/2015/06/Debate-e-book-small.pdf

and most vulnerable embers of our society are taken away to death under the covering of "law".

Well, it is true the courts haven't overturned *Roe v Wade*. But it is more accurate to say that they haven't overturned it *yet*. What if antebellum abolitionists had applied these same standards back in the day? In 1805? 1835? 1855? What would their response have been if some "Super Abolitionists" popped up in the 1840s and criticized the work of Wilberforce and Garrison as compromised and ineffectual? It took the abolitionists 80 years and their work did not end in revival, but in Civil War. Legislative agreements like the Missouri Compromise and the Compromise of 1850 did not end slavery but helped to further isolate the American south and stop the progression of slavery westward. One only can engage in some alternative history to see the wisdom involved.

Let's do a thought experiment. It is the year 1849. California is admitted to the Union as a slave state. Ten years later, with war breaking out, it would have been next to

impossible for the Union to subdue California with its gigantic

territory and vast coastline. The entire coast would have been

buffeted with British ships helping with the Confederate cause.

We know this because of the British support of the southern

states throughout the Civil War. Thank God, this did not

happen. So logically, *incrementalism saved the Union and helped*

to end slavery.

If Abolish Human Abortion's acolytes were around back

then, one wonders on which side they would have fought.

12. *"The fact is that numerous pro-life candidates have been*

   elected over the past forty-two years, well over 200 pro-life

   laws and regulations have been passed, and the right to

   murder one's own children while they are in the womb

   remains legal in every state of the union."

True, abortion is still legal. But pro-life laws and these

regulations have saved lives. Closed clinics equals saved lives.

Limits to abortion access equals saved lives. Yes, abortion should be and will be illegal and unthinkable one day, Lord willing. But when 50 abortion clinics are closing every year, we are winning. At this rate, there will be zero abortion clinics in 10-12 years. We wish that abortion would disappear today. Every dead child is a tragedy. But we must keep our eye on the ball here. We must follow the examples of those who shined His light in the darkness before us.

AHA mocks those who advocate "regulating" abortion. Yet regulating public health funding across the country has had great effect in reducing the number of abortions.

Let's look at more of Dr. New's research. From 1980-1995, North Carolina publicly funded abortion for low-income women. But when funds ran out, there were statistically significant decreases in the abortion rate. Months later, a statistically significant increase in the birth rate was found. And, when looking at the rates in the black community, 37% of abortion-vulnerable women facing an unplanned pregnancy carried their baby to term when funding was not available. [13]

What should our response be to statistics like these? Should we refuse to rejoice because abortion is still legal, or should we shout hallelujah? I can rejoice in this. I can shout it out loud. More lives were saved because of this and other legislative victories!

13. *"The establishment of justice and the practice of pure and undefiled religion has been given over to a coalition of syncretists who not only prefer the worldly wisdom of man to the word of God, but also yoke themselves together with those who want to make a career of saving babies regardless of whether or not they love God or possess a worldview capable of grounding ethics and morality."*

In logic and rhetoric, there is a fallacy called a straw man.

A straw man argument is an easily-defeatable argument that is

[13] Ibid, p. 72

similar to the argument your interlocutor actually made. Straw

men are easily defeated because they attack a weaker version of

the argument than the actual argument. Suppose a politician says,

"My opponent is opposed to my health care plan, because he

wants old people to die." Of course his opponent doesn't want

people to die. The mischaracterization of your opponent's

position is a straw man. It is easily knocked over.

AHA loves the straw man, but the above sentiment is

almost too much. Religion is compromised and worldly? The

church is compromised for supporting pro-life groups and

individuals? According to them, Abolish Human Abortion is the

only pure organization (non-organization).

In the New Testament we are given Luke 9:49-50 (NKJV).

"Now John answered and said, "Master, we saw

someone casting out demons in Your Name, and we forbade him

because he does not follow with us." But Jesus said to him, "Do not forbid him, for he who is not against us is on our side." John

played the sectarianism card with Jesus, thinking that Jesus would

care about some non-approved demon casters in Israel. Jesus

didn't care, because He knew that anyone casting out a demon is

not an enemy of the Kingdom of God.

Still purists abound, or more accurately—the self-righteous

sectarians-- and they have been around for a while. See Numbers

11.

[24] So Moses went out and told the people the words of

the LORD, and he gathered the seventy men of the elders of the

people and placed them around the tabernacle. [25] Then

the LORD came down in the cloud, and spoke to him, and took

of the Spirit that *was* upon him, and placed *the same* upon the

seventy elders; and it happened, when the Spirit rested upon

them, that they prophesied, although they never did *so* again.[b]

[26] But two men had remained in the camp: the name of

one *was* Eldad, and the name of the other Medad. And the Spirit

rested upon them. Now they *were* among those listed, but who had not gone out to the tabernacle; yet they prophesied in the camp. [27] And a young man ran and told Moses, and said, "Eldad and Medad are prophesying in the camp." [28] So Joshua the son of Nun, Moses' assistant, *one* of his choice men, answered and said, "Moses my lord, forbid them!" [29] Then Moses said to him, "Are you zealous for my sake? Oh, that all the LORD's people were prophets *and* that the LORD would put His Spirit upon them!" [30] And Moses returned to the camp, he and the elders of Israel." (Numbers 11:24-30)

Notice how Moses was approached by some zealous sectarians. These guys did not want anyone to prophecy unless they had been previously approved by the Moses-Aaron leadership team. But Moses did not see this as a problem. He said, "Oh, that all Israel would prophecy." Moses wanted more people to prophesy, not less. Moses wanted more people to hear from the LORD and to proclaim the LORD's words to others. Moses was not a purist. He was not a sectarian. He had seen enough division and selfishness and whining among the Israelites.

He was rejoicing that others were hearing from the Lord.

As we look back at AHA's statement, I have a loaded question of my own. Who wants to "make a career" out of saving babies? All the sidewalk counselors and PCC (pregnancy care centers) workers and activists that I know would give ANYTHING to NOT have to do what we do. I involve myself in this statement, too. For Abolish Human Abortion to claim that anyone who works across denominational or political lines is a worldly compromised syncretist is just wrong. AHA constantly impugns the motives of millions of hardworking Christians. Paul tells us in 1 Corinthians 13 to believe the best about our brothers and sisters in Christ. James tells us not to judge others (James 4:11-12).

Abolish Human Abortion should repent of impugning the motives of all pro-life workers who do not agree with their methods, since many of these workers were in the ministry of saving babies' lives for years before many of us were born.

14. *"Many of them are opportunists who have lost their faith and trust in God. They continue to profess their personal Christian piety and beliefs while they pander to the religious bodies of the land for financial support and approval."*

How in the world could the AHA organization-non-organization make a statement like this? Is there any evidence for this? Anywhere? What percentage of sidewalk counselors and PCC directors have lost their faith in God? People lose their faith all the time. But I would argue that the work of a pregnancy care center director or a sidewalk counselor is an odd career for someone who has lost their faith in God.

As for the shot they take at fundraising, AHA claims that they do not do any fundraising. Yet they run the site ahagear.com which provides materials and clothing for the movement. [14] There

is nothing wrong with this, of course. However, it is hypocritical

---

[14] Ahagear.org

to condemn Christians for fundraising efforts when a) they do it too and b) no biblical directive exists against fundraising. In fact, Paul mentions fundraising in his letter to the Philippians, which he recounts the Thessalonian support of his ministry (Phil. 4:10-19).

15. *"They approach the "issue" of abortion from a secular and pluralistic standpoint, denying the power of the Gospel as having anything to do with the fight against abortion except, perhaps, as a secondary issue that might come up during "saving the babies."*

` This is basically another straw man. Remember, AHA loves to argue this way. Who are they talking about? Who denies the power of the gospel? With this standard, Abolish Human Abortion slanders entire groups of people and makes several hasty generalizations. Again, think about the committed pro-lifers you know in your church. Ask them about their methods. Does Jesus ever come up in their ministry at the clinics? I am pretty sure it does. Remember that AHA is the organization/non-organization with proven biblical inconsistencies. Furthermore, Christians are called to believe the best about our brothers and sisters in Christ (1 Cor. 13) and not tear them down (Eph. 4:28-29). Here we see examples of both AHA's bad "roots" and bad "fruits."

Let's keep knocking down those straw men. What percentage of people have lost their faith? 10%? 40%? To paraphrase one of their common questions, "what does losing your faith look like in a culture that practices child sacrifice?" These are questions that Abolish Human Abortion cannot answer.

Sidewalk counseling is a strange way to lose your faith. So is starting a pregnancy care center or a pro-life political organization. But it makes perfect sense to AHA, or at least they want you to think so. It is another illogical argument grown from bad roots.

16. *"Local pro-life churches in America have by and large attempted to put band aids on the pervasive practice of child sacrifice...they have chosen not to call the nation to repent, but instead to vote, to send money, attend this or that yearly event, and choose life for themselves. They have not failed to be pro-life ...they have failed to be Christian."*

I don't even know where to start. This is almost laughable. It's not a sentiment. It's more like a conniption fit.

Imagine a spoiled high school student writing a poem for open mic night. She reads it while truculently slapping the hair out of her face as mom films the whole thing. Afterward, she then drops the mic, thinking herself profound. People are too polite to tell her that she isn't good at poetry and needs to do something else with her life. Too bad American Idol's Simon Cowell wasn't there.

I digress. According to Abolish Human Abortion,

pregnancy centers fail to be Christian! Sidewalk counselors fail to be Christian! Pro-life pastors are failing to be Christian! Everyone except the AHA organization-non-organization is failing to be Christian. Let's examine this for a moment. This also means Paul failed to be Christian because he did not protest the social ills of the Roman Empire the same way AHA does. The apostles failed to be Christian too, because they did not call the entire nation of Rome to repent. Paul and the apostles did the apparently less important work of preaching the gospel and building churches. Oh, and Jesus also failed to be Christian because He did not go to Rome and rebuke the wickedness of the Roman empire and advance social justice. It is so easy to see AHA's biblical confusion. No one can meet the standards they are setting up for others to meet.

Further, what does calling the nation to repent mean? How do you know when the nation has repented? I agree that revival and repentance in the church are necessary, but revival and repentance are gospel issues (first) and pro-life activism issues (second). Does calling the nation repent mean street preaching and evangelism? Does it mean church planting? If it does, shouldn't you believe in a local church first?

Yes, our nation needs to repent. But repentance is a gift of God (Rom. 2). Our faith is a gift (Eph. 2). We love because He first loved us (John 15).

The whole idea of national repentance is theologically tricky. If a nation outlaws child sacrifice, does that mean that nation is automatically Christian? Of course not. Tell that to the countries of Malta, Nicaragua, and Chile, all of whom have outlawed abortion but without any real Christian reformation that can be seen. According to Abolish Human Abortion, these nations should be hotbeds of biblical righteousness? Are they? Not even close. Should we be expecting the next Reformation to be taking place there? No.

Afghanistan has also outlawed abortion throughout its history, does this mean that it has repented? No, it means that it is 99.2% Muslim and strictly adheres to the Quran.

AHA's arguments are very misleading and erroneous. When they say, *if the gospel goes forth, abortion will end.* Maybe. The gospel should go forth. And it will. But as history shows us, many nations have stricter abortion laws, who have nowhere near the Christian influence of the United States.

Abortion is illegal in many countries, but it is not illegal in those countries because of the gospel. In the United States, when we believe that abortion should be illegal, it will be made so by our elected representatives. How will it be made illegal? By passing laws that outlaw it. Who makes the laws? The legislative branch. Who elects legislators? The people. Which people? Just the righteous ones? No. Is this going to happen anytime soon?

Probably not. Why? *Because the American people do not want it to end yet.* By God's grace, one day, they will.

17. *"As abolitionists, we refuse to go with the multitude to do evil, and we are determined to never commit or concede any evil in order that good may come. We believe that God never requires us to support lesser evils to secure greater goods." (Ex. 23:2; Rom. 3:8)*

The verses that Abolish Human Abortion cite here are out of context. The Exodus passage is discussing a legal proceeding where people may be tempted to follow the majority opinion. It has nothing to do with working with others to cure a social evil like slavery or abortion. The Romans passage references those who are abusing the grace of God in not fighting remaining sin in their lives and likewise questioning the justice and mercy of God.

Let's discuss their point about means and ends. For the

sake of argument, let's assert that God never uses evil means. If this is true, then the Bible contradicts itself. God uses all nations to accomplish his will. He didn't wait for Israel to get their act together, He sent them a pagan king named Cyrus as a liberator. Isaiah 45 calls Cyrus the anointed one. God used Pharaoh to achieve his ends (Exodus 7) God used the Canaanite prostitute Rahab (Joshua 2). He used Babylon to punish Israel (Jer. 28). God used Nebuchadnezzar as well (Daniel 3).

It is God's world. He can use pagan kings and prostitutes to accomplish His plan. He is sovereign. He ordains all things. He ordains the means and the ends.

Is Abolish Human Abortion really saying that Garrison, Wilberforce or Martin Luther King only accepted help from Christians? Was the abolitionist movement purely a movement of the church? That would be a very difficult argument to make for AHA. Think about recent American history. Were the Allied forces guilty of compromise when the USSR joined their ranks in fighting the Nazis? Should every Allied soldier have just quit because the USSR was violently advancing communism? Or were they correct to join against the common cause of defeating the Nazis?

God uses evil people all the time to accomplish His purposes (Acts 2:23). God judges and uses the nations for His glory, as Stephen so eloquently recounted (Acts 7).

To assume that God can't or won't use certain people in the fight against abortion is not only biblically ignorant, but severely limiting of God's power. And it is saying AHA's way is better than God's. Talk about bad fruit. It is starting to smell.

18. *"As abolitionists, we believe that measures only designed to outlaw specific methods of killing some preborn beings, while abandoning many others to destruction, are ignorant, perverse, and dishonoring to God."*

Fine, then babies will continue to die. Abolish Human Abortion essentially says *either save all the babies or let them all die*. Would William Lloyd Garrison or William Wilberforce advocate for this kind of fallacious "either-or" thinking? Either free every slave or free no slave? Would abolitionists during the antebellum era in America have resisted the underground railroad because it didn't save all the runaway slaves? Never. Would they have opposed legislation that outlawed slavery in some of the newly formed United States, in order to get the slave states cornered and surrounded by anti-slavery states? No. They used pragmatic steps to achieve their ideological goals.

Is ending abortion a war? A titanic struggle? Yes.

We need to grow up and learn some principles for battle.

Abolish Human Abortion incorrectly argues that the only reason abortion is still legal in the United States is that "pro-lifers" have the power to stop abortion but either cannot or will not, do it. This is a straw man! We don't live in a dictatorship where the King or Pharoah can simply end abortion by regal fiat. We live in a constitutional republic where we vote for those whom we wish to represent us.

And as we have voted, those votes have made a difference. Dr. Michael New found in his research that parental involvement laws and informed consent laws *reduce the rate of abortions.* Nineteen different studies demonstrate that parental involvement laws lead to a statistically significant reduction in the in-state minor abortion rate anywhere from 13% to 42%, with most in the 15%-20% range. [15]

More babies are alive because of these incremental steps. But don't wait for AHA to celebrate. They call this ignorant, perverse, and dishonoring to God.

---

[15] Ibid, p. 73

19. "Today's pro—life establishment is focused on making abortion safer, cleaner, and possibly more rare."

This is absolutely false, insulting and offensive. Pro-life legislation is a means to an end. Think about this for a second. Abolition Human Abortion expects the same culture that legalized abortion to outlaw it. This is not going to happen. Rather, we must take what the culture gives us because everyone over the age of 18 in the United States of America has the right to vote. We do not live in 1630 anymore. Abolish Human Abortion refuses to promote "incremental" legislation but we know incremental legislations can shift opinions, challenge previous court decisions, and save lives. We should celebrate every saved life as a victory.

If a policeman can be called to stop one murder, is he a failure because he couldn't stop all the murders? He might as well stop trying until he is sure of complete success, no?

Does a firefighter not try to save as many people as he can

from a burning building because he may not be able to save them all? He should compromise and stay home, right?

Of course not. But AHA calls these questions straw men because they have no good answer for them. Their arguments are illogical; they are grounded by the bad roots of self-righteousness and hostility to the church which continues to produce the bad fruits of confusion and division.

19. "The focus of the pro-life movement has been the regulation of child sacrifice."

Regulation? No. Years of incremental steps toward the goal of ending abortion? Yes. Total abortion bans have not passed a single statehouse or in the U.S. Congress. Essentially, Abolish Human Abortion is saying until you can outlaw it, do nothing. Would the abolitionists that AHA rightly revere be called compromisers for regulating slave ships like William Wilberforce did? One wonders.

Abolish Human Abortion argues that any regulation of

abortion is compromise, but the regulating of abortion has led to many saved babies. Former Florida House Representative Charles Van Zant offered up a total abortion ban every year in the Florida Legislature and every year it did not pass. In our current climate, shouldn't lawmakers focus rightly on getting as many regulations as they can because they save lives? Regulations equal restrictions and restrictions mean more abortion vulnerable women will chose to keep their babies than without these regulations.

Even in a state like Mississippi which has only one abortion clinic, a federal judge blocked its closure despite a ban passed by the Mississippi House and Senate and signed by the Governor. Americans do not want to outlaw abortion—yet. But incremental legislation is changing minds and saving lives.

As I write this, I am sitting in a studio apartment in downtown St. Petersburg after Hurricane Irma has wiped out the power at our home and to almost 400,000 residents in Pinellas County. Stories are beginning to emerge of first responders who heroically put their lives on the line for their fellow citizens. Residents were rescued from high waters, fires, and flying debris. We survived the storm, but it caused me to think.

If my house is flooding, and an atheist pulls up in a boat and offers to rescue me and my family, I am not going to press his ideology of saving lives and how it contrasts with his view of natural selection. **I am glad he is there.**

These are the battle principles that AHA needs to learn. We need each other. We need all hands on deck. We need allies and not enemies in this war. For as Abolish Human Abortion often rightly declares, lives are at stake.

20. *"In their misguided attempt to protect "as many babies as they can" they have thoughtlessly abandoned the many for the few and undermined the very foundation for their*

demands. In hopes of "saving some" the pro-life movement

has continually made exceptions that inadvertently deny the

protection of all."

False, again. See the all or nothing approach to AHA?

Imagine the Coast Guard needing to save 500 people drowning

on a cruise ship. However, they refuse to go because they only

have 200 life rafts. That would be a horrible tragedy. They could

have saved 200 lives. But instead all 500 people perish. How sad.

But the Abolish Human Abortion argument against

incrementalism is actually worse. What if the Coast Guard's

refusal to help those who are savable was hailed as

uncompromising bravery? That would be messed up. Right? But

that's exactly what Abolish Human Abortion is advocating.

It's 2019. Our culture has not repented. Over half of

Americans hold biblically inconsistent views on marriage.

Millions still approve of abortion on demand. Pornography and promiscuity are everywhere. We are entertained by blood, filth, and sex. We are not a culture that has repented yet. Abortion will not end now. Not yet. Similarly, in 1846, the US was not going to outlaw slavery. In 1780, the British House of Commons was not going to abolish the slave trade. Today, we are not able to save every baby. But we can save some.

One day God may move in the hearts of His people to end abortion. He may not. He may allow us to go deeper into rebellion and destruction. Our nation may repent. It may dissolve into Civil War. But this God's business, not ours. Unless we repent, we will not see revival. This revival might lead to the outlawing of abortion. Or it might not.

We just have to be faithful.

21. *"The overall effect of the movement's work has been to inculcate pessimism, entrench godless pragmatism, and perpetuate the idea that abolition is impossible."*

This is actually quite rich. The charge of pessimism is hilarious, given that the pro-life movement which AHA ridicules is the same movement that, much to AHA's scorn, tries to save as many babies as possible. This is not pessimism. *Pro-lifers* believe that even a non-believer can be opposed to the abortion holocaust. *Pro-lifers believe that we must* work with other believers across denominational lines. *Pro-lifers believe* in common grace, that all truth is God's truth and you need not necessarily be a born-again Christian to oppose abortion. This is not pessimism, it's actually optimism. The pro-life movement, while not perfection, is bearing good fruits, but Abolish Human Abortion fails to recognize them.

This particular form of pragmatism is not godless. Remember that everyone is a pragmatist, seeking to practice their ideology. It is far more pessimistic and godless to insist *every baby* to be saved from abortion until we can save *one baby* from abortion.

22. *"Stop approaching abortion as though it were health care,*

and stop trying to close down abortion mills because they fail

to meet the medical establishment's code of cleanliness."

Wait, what? This is another example of poor reasoning

on the part of AHA. No one is saying this. However, if medical

cleanliness standards help close clinics down, then why does

Abolish Human Abortion oppose them? Because the clinics are

closed by a means other than a total abortion ban? Ridiculous.

23. *"Stop acting as if justice can be established by passing a*

law which demands a mother view her child on an

ultrasound screen prior to having him or her killed."

I don't know of any pro-life advocate who is completely

satisfied when an ultrasound bill gets passed. No one stops

working toward the ultimate goal. We all know that an ultrasound

bill is not the same as ending abortion. But pro-life advocates know ultrasound bills have saved lives. It is easy to see this

dangerous false choice in the above quote from #24 that AHA is

so fond of promoting. The fact is that ultrasound laws have

worked. How have they worked? They have saved babies. They

have saved lives. Have they saved every life? No, but they have

saved some. Did the Underground Railroad save every slave?

No, but it saved some. The parallel is the same.

Again, let's cite Dr. New's research as proof that incremental

legislation saves lives. In 1992, Pennsylvania Governor Robert

Casey, who might have been the last pro-life Democrat of a

national stature in the United States, signed an informed consent

bill into law. The law required women to look at color photos of

their preborn babies. Research shows that women who saw the
color photos were 2% to 7% less likely to abort their babies. [16]

These may seem like small or insignificant numbers, but these

are human beings, made in God's image, who are alive today

---

[16] Ibid, p. 53

because of this legislation. Every saved life is a victory.

In a state the size of Pennsylvania, these numbers equal thousands of saved babies. But AHA refuses to promote any incremental legislation and claims that those who do are compromised. Here we see more of their bad roots and bad fruits. Tell that to the thousands of babies saved because of these laws. It is completely illogical to try and argue that these incrementalist restrictions on abortion are bad things.

24. *"We call upon pro-lifers to stop focusing the bulk of their time and energy on creating, funding, and promoting pregnancy centers that operate under the false paradigm of "choice."*

Now, stuff starts to get real, as the kids say. We see clearly AHA's real adversaries. The real enemy is....Planned Parenthood? The Democratic Party? Compromised pro-abortion churches? No. The real enemy is the entire *pro-life movement.* According to them, pro-lifers are the problem. And what is the crime of the broader pro-life movement? Well, despite the fact that babies are saved in pregnancy care centers, the crime to Abolish Human Abortion is that pregnancy centers raise funds and exist. They have buildings and staff and necessary supplies that cost money and they use the funds they raise to get and keep these things—to save lives.

Here in the Tampa Bay area we have one of the largest pregnancy center networks in the United States. In the last three years, New Life Solutions has saved over 1,000 babies from abortion in this high traffic abortion area. And this is a problem for AHA? One wonders why.

Because they have a different method that AHA? Because they haven't saved every baby in the Tampa Bay area? This is bizarre and illogical.

Abolish Human Abortion doesn't take too kindly to pregnancy centers. AHA has developed a false impression that pro-life pregnancy centers are either not religious or religiously neutral. In other words, if a pregnancy care center employee does not immediately begin rebuking the abortion-vulnerable mother for her sinful choices and her murderous heart, they are compromising the truth of the gospel. But again, they are confusing the issue here.

What is this battle about? If this is a battle to save the life of the baby, and to provide an environment where the woman will save her child, then using language under the paradigm of choice is not false. It's strategic. If a woman won't hear the Bible, but will hear about her choice, her baby might be saved. What is the problem here? Paul declared that he wanted to be "all things to all people that he might save some" (1 Cor. 9:19-23). This was also a strategic position. Paul was used to shine light in the darkness. Paul was firmly rooted in the gospel and his God honoring methods bore good fruit.

But if you view this as a battle to see how much truth can be proclaimed to the abortion vulnerable woman, and if you perceive yourself as a modern-day Elijah—then saving the baby's life is secondary. Your priority is to rebuke her as much as you can before she runs across the street to the abortion clinic where at least people will be kind to her. This is not good, biblical, God-honoring. This is self-righteousness. This is very bad fruit.

There are countless pro-life pregnancy care centers (PCCs) who do proclaim the truth of the gospel and work with women regardless of their spiritual state. The truth is proclaimed in a compassionate way. Babies are saved. Women and men hear the gospel and are transformed. Sadly, this still isn't enough for AHA.

26. *"Pro-lifers must cease making deals with Moloch, entreating him to clean up his child sacrifice centers, widen their hallways, or bring them closer to the places where*

wanted babies are born. Pro-lifers must cease to stand before Pharaoh declaring, "Let....some of my people go."

Again we see the false dichotomy. We aren't in 1200 BC. We don't make appeals to Pharaoh. We don't have a Pharaoh. We have a constitutional republic. We have a Supreme Court. So, the Pharaoh analogy breaks down. Imagine if the President outlawed abortion by executive order. It would be challenged immediately by every lower court. The next President could reverse it. It would be overthrown. And it would cost the pro-life movement precious time and resources, to say nothing of the gains we have had throughout the past 20 years that would ultimately be lost.

The Pharaoh analogy presents a problem too. For it was God who hardened Pharaoh's heart. God who had to break Pharaoh to accomplish his eternal purposes (Exodus 10). It would not have mattered to Pharaoh if the entire nation of Israel had stood before him with signs. God had to do the work. And what's more, Pharoah was not told to repent, he was just told to let the Israelites go!

Now we must wrestle with the Moloch comment. For those of you who need an introduction to the demonic Canaanite god, Moloch was the god of child sacrifice, demanding children to be cast into the fire, while Moloch's agents stood at the sides of the flames blowing trumpets to drown out the cries of the infants as they burned alive.

Evil. Wicked. Moloch.

I've been called some names in my life. I am certainly not perfect. In fact, I'm one of the biggest sinners I know. But I can say I have never made a deal with Moloch. I don't have any trumpets. I enjoy a nice campfire. But I always make sure the infants in the area are good distance away.

To say AHA has a rhetorical image problem is like saying the guy on "Hoarders" needs a trash can.

27. "We call pro-lifers to reject all compromise and join us in calling our nation to repent of the sin of child sacrifice. We call the pro-life movement to repent."

I applaud AHA for their clarity in this statement. I disagree with it, but at least AHA is honestly proclaiming who they view as the real enemy. The real enemy is the pro-life movement. Not Planned Parenthood. Not Democratic politicians who have protected abortion on demand since 1992. Not compromised churches who support abortion. But the pro-lifers, the pregnancy centers, the sidewalk counselors, and those who have prayed without ceasing to end for over 40 years, are the real problem. No. I call on Abolish Human Abortion to reject their divisive and unbiblical methods and repent of their misguided zeal.

28. "We will show this nation what it is they approve, allow and ignore, and what future generations will remember them for approving, allowing and ignoring."

Fair enough, but it is precisely this culture that AHA then expects to outlaw abortion. They also show themselves agitating and picking fights with other Christians instead of living out the gospel with grace and love.

Abolish Human Abortion often promotes graphic images of aborted babies in public and cite Ephesians 5:11 for support. I do not necessarily disagree with them. I remember the effect that it had on me and on others back in 1999 at the University of Idaho. I can testify to their good use. But I think they should be used sparingly, on college campuses, and maybe high school classrooms, not necessarily on any random street corner.

29. "We shall not think, speak or write, with moderation."

These actual words come from William Lloyd Garrison, the abolitionist. It's a good thought, but the Apostle Paul outranks even Garrison. Read Paul's words in Colossians 3:8-16.

"But now you yourselves are to put off all these: anger, wrath, malice, blasphemy, filthy language out of your mouth. [9] Do not lie to one another, since you have put off the old man with his deeds, [10] and have put on the new *man* who is renewed in knowledge according to the image of Him who created him, [11] where there is neither Greek nor Jew, circumcised nor uncircumcised, barbarian, Scythian, slave *nor* free, but Christ *is* all and in all. Therefore, as *the* elect of God, holy and beloved, put on tender mercies, kindness, humility, meekness, longsuffering; [13] bearing with one another, and forgiving one another, if anyone has a complaint against another; even as Christ forgave you, so you also *must do.* [14] But above all these things put on love, which is the bond of perfection. [15] And let the peace of God rule in your hearts, to which also you were called in one body; and be thankful. [16] Let the word of Christ dwell in you richly in all wisdom, teaching and admonishing one another in psalms and hymns and spiritual songs, singing with grace in your hearts to the Lord. [17] And whatever you do in word or deed, *do* all in the name of the Lord Jesus, giving thanks to God the Father through Him."

Christians should act like Christians. Christians should be "rooted" in the gospel and bringing forth good "fruit".

30. "We are not attacking the Bride of Christ in any way. Rather, we are exhorting all believers everywhere to be the church and to boldly practice true and vital Christianity in the midst of a culture that kills its children."

Actually, Abolish Human Abortion *is* attacking the church. Calling her compromised with Moloch and saying that she has inaugurated Satan sounds like attacking language to me. It is difficult to imagine a more strongly worded attack. Christians should not talk this way about other Christians. It sounds more like unhinged lunacy than biblical exhortation. And it hurts the overall message of the pro-life movement.

31. "By the blood of the lamb and the word of our witness, by the power of the Holy Spirit, in His Providence and in accordance with His plan, we shall crush the dragon abortion beneath our feet. (Rev. 12:11; Rom. 16:20)

This is extremely poor exegesis. This almost sounds like a

faith healer like Benny Hinn or some other "name it, claim it" hoohaw.

Abortion is not the devil. It is one of the works of the devil. Sex trafficking is not the devil. It is one of the works of the devil. Racism is not the devil. It is one of the works of the devil. In fact, James tells us that thinking too highly of ourselves is sensual and demonic as well (James 3:15).

This is not to say that Christians do not have a responsibility to end abortion. We most certainly do. But personifying abortion with Satan himself is a bridge too far. Ending abortion is not the gospel! But those of us who believe the gospel should rescue the perishing as we are told to in Proverbs 24:11-12.

The roots of AHA are found in an amalgam of anti-slavery abolitionism of the 19th century combined with robust sin-seeking salvos of Elijah or Ezekiel. The roots are bad. The fruit is bad too.

In chapter nine we will discuss more about how the church can do more to end abortion.

CHAPTER FIVE: NO SPECIAL CALLING?

The AHA website has the following on one of its pages. The quote is lengthy and I have underlined and boldfaced the parts that we will discuss further.

> *"WE DO NOT WANT YOUR MONEY.....In fact, we do not even take donations, nor do we possess a formal organization or staff whom we have to pay.* **We are not looking for financial support, admiration or approval.** *We have not produced this website to put our exploits on display and then ask you to help us to make a financial donation to "our cause".* **We believe that the abolition of human abortion is an obligation of the people of God and we are calling on all people who know the Living God to rise up and do exploits in unity as His Body and Helpmate (sic) Bride (Daniel 11:32, Rev. 12:11).**

*We have built this website for the same reason we do everything else; to bring glory to God and bring the Gospel of His Kingdom into conflict with the evil of our age. We are seeking to fulfill the great commission and make disciples of Jesus who obey His commands and proclaim the good news of His Kingdom in a culture that kills its children. All we ask is that you examine our views and actions in the light of God's word and respond to what you have seen and heard with humility, the fear of God (and not man!) and practice spiritual discernment. **<u>We are not asking you to join us, fund us, or to do exactly what we do, but we believe that the Church of the Living God is rising up against child sacrifice and that all believers should unify together in the cause of Christ and work to establish justice for the preborn in His name. This work requires no special calling, ordination or permission, all that is required has been made available through Christ's death and resurrection and through the indwelling of His</u>***

Holy Spirit. Walk in obedience to Him. He will help you know what to do. To join your brothers and sisters in the work, please contact us by clicking here." [17]

I will take each of these statements one at a time.

1. *We are not looking for financial support, admiration or approval.*

If you click on the link labeled AHA Gear, you see numerous shirts and items for sale all portraying the AHA logo. There is nothing wrong with this. If this is how Harmon and Hunter and others make a living, fine. There is no reason to be shy about fundraising. Every nonprofit must solicit donors to ensure their success. Abolish Human Abortion should just embrace the fact that they have an organization and have bills to pay. It is dishonest to cloak their intentions. It is divisive to criticize other pro-life organizations who fundraise.

---

[17] Abolishhumanabortion.com

2. We believe that the abolition of human abortion is an obligation of the people of God and we are calling on all people who know the Living God to rise up and do exploits in unity as His Body and Helpmate Bride (sic) (Daniel 11:32, Rev. 12:11).

A couple things here. First, we can say amen to the fact that all Christians should rise and up and do exploits. Yes, amen. We agree that we should be unified, as Christ prayed in John 17. However, from all the rhetoric that AHA spews about other Christians being compromised and how we have inaugurated Satan, and how we have sold out to Moloch, Abolish Human Abortion should stop being surprised when the average Christian runs from them. They are not seeking unity. They are seeking division.

Secondly, in order to strive for unity, we should be a part of the local church, not just the universal church. The "universal church" is not good enough for the fellowship,

108

worship, and accountability that the New Testament requires.

The local church, with local elders and deacons, and local

fellowship, will provide this unity that AHA rightly longs for.

Thirdly, Abolish Human Abortion isolates themselves by not

working with the local church. If every AHA adherent joined a

conservative Christ-centered church, submitted to their

leadership, and served their brothers and sisters, their influence

would grow exponentially.

3. *We are not asking you to join us, fund us, or to do exactly what we do, but we believe that the Church of the Living God is rising up against child sacrifice and that all believers should unify together in the cause of Christ and work to establish justice for the preborn in His name.*

I have personal experience with the first part of #3

being absolutely false. Of course they are asking everyone to join

them. They need to be more honest about this. There is nothing

wrong with starting a website or a movement. Just be honest

about your intentions. Does AHA really want unity with other believers? It's an honest question, because when a pro-lifer disagrees with them, advocates of Abolish Human Abortion calls them compromised apostates whose arguments are all straw men. Pro-lifers are said to be deceived by the inauguration of Satan. And don't forget all those secret deals AHA accuses pro-lifers of making with Moloch. So, while this statement is a good goal for Abolish Human Abortion, most people who have any experience with them at all don't experience this when they come face to face with them. Their bad roots will never produce unifying fruits.

4. _**This work requires no special calling, ordination or permission, all that is required has been made available through Christ's death and resurrection and through the indwelling of His Holy Spirit. Walk in obedience to Him. He will help you know what to do.**_

Here we see some of Abolish Human Abortion's greatest theological confusion. While I do not doubt their intentions, we still have to measure them against Scripture. It looks as if part of the confusion comes in the first part of #4, especially the sentence "all that is required has been made available through Christ's death and resurrection and through the indwelling of His Holy Spirit." Now, this is true as it relates to salvation. If you took out the phrase "all that is required" and replaced it with "salvation" then there is no quarrel with AHA.

However, salvation *alone* does not equip the Christian for every good work. We must not overlook the Holy Spirit and His gifts. Some Christians are gifted to be pastors, evangelists, some are called to be teachers, some are called to fill other roles to serve the body of Christ. This is basic Christian doctrine in 1 Corinthians 12, Ephesians 4, 1 Timothy 2 and Titus 2. We share the same faith but not necessarily the same gifts. Not everyone has the same ability or gift from God. In fact, Paul says this explicitly in 1 Corinthians 12.

"If the foot should say, "Because I am not a hand, I am not

of the body," is it therefore not of the body? And if the ear should

say, "Because I am not an eye, I am not of the body," is it therefore

not of the body? If the whole body *were* an eye, where *would be* the

hearing? If the whole *were* hearing, where *would be* the

smelling? But now God has set the members, each one of them, in

the body just as He pleased. And if they were all one member,

where *would* the body *be?*" (1 Cor. 12:15-19)

Missionary work—essentially the work where AHA finds

themselves—absolutely requires a special calling from God,

testified to by the elders of a local church. Abolish Human

Abortion's views are biblically inconsistent.

Furthermore, Abolish Human Abortion needs to

temper themselves. Nowhere Christians need to be more careful

with the tone and tenor of our behavior than in the area of pro-

life ministry. This does not mean we compromise. But just like

Paul, we shine the light of the gospel into the darkness with the

love of Christ. Self-righteous condemnations and divisive name calling have no place in advancing the mission. We should all be more self-aware in the pro-life movement. Not only are we swimming in deep counter cultural waters—we are speaking to an audience with deep scars since 25% of women between the ages of 18 and 49 are post-abortive. [18]

A personal story might help. I find more people outside the church think what I do as a sidewalk counselor is brave and commendable than those inside most churches. Many Christians have negative images in their heads of front-lines pro-life ministry. I have to constantly explain what I am *not doing* to most church people. This is part of the reality but we need to be more aware of ourselves, realizing that it is Jesus we are representing. Sadly, Abolish Human Abortion contributes to this problem with their lone ranger, Elijah complex.

Their bad "roots" have grown bad "fruits" that damage the

---

[18] https://www.guttmacher.org/news-release/2017/abortion-common-experience-us-women-despite-dramatic-declines-rates

way pro-life ministries are perceived. AHA must repent of their

lone-ranger mentality and begin to accommodate themselves to

the larger body of Christ. They are not currently bearing good

fruit, because their doctrinal roots are confused and immature.

CHAPTER SIX:
AHA'S MISLEADING, CULTISH TERMINOLOGY

I really did not want to have to write this chapter.

Really.

Discussing any group as a potential "cult" is always a bit problematic, let me say at the outset that I do not use the term cult pejoratively, but as an actual definition that describes specific groups of people. *I do believe,* however, that there are sincere Christians involved with Abolish Human Abortion. This criticism and analysis of AHA's cultishness is done with all of this in mind. I know that Abolish Human Abortion does not consider themselves to be a cult, but then again, Scripture should be our standard.

The late great Walter R. Martin wrote *The Kingdom of the Cults* in 1965 as a theological handbook for Christians seeking to understand non-Christian cults. In this chapter, I will be referring to Dr. Martin's work as I compare AHA to Scripture. Martin argues in his introduction—

"By cultism we mean the adherence to doctrines which are pointedly contradictory to orthodox Christianity and which yet claim the distinction of either tracing their origin to orthodox sources or of being in essential harmony with those sources. Cultism, in short, is any *major deviation from orthodox Christianity relative to the cardinal doctrines of the Christian faith.*" *(emphasis mine)*

Martin continues, "One of the most potent tools, [that the cultist has] is theological term switching. Through the manipulation of terminology, it is therefore obvious that the cultist has the Christian at a distinct disadvantage, *particularly in the realm of the great fundamental doctrines*

---

[19] Martin, Walter R. The Kingdom of the Cults. Bethany Fellowship, Inc. Publishers. Minneapolis, MN, 1965, p. 18-21

of *Biblical theology.*"[19]

Let's analyze this in several different areas.

1. Pro-life vs. Abolitionism

As we've discovered, AHA is not pro-life. They reject the pro-life label. They are hostile to the pro-life movement. They have adopted the terminology of abolitionism instead of pro-life. Abolish Human Abortion divides the pro-life movement into two categories. Anyone who is pro-life is not an abolitionist. Abolitionists are the true followers of Jesus. Pro-lifers have *"failed to be Christian"* according to the Declaration of Abolitionist Principles.

But why does AHA seek to diminish the work of over 40 plus years of principled, pro-life work? And why they have worked so hard to create this distinction? They appear to seek unnecessary division where unity is so desperately needed. What's more, by ignoring or seeking to invalidate the pro-life victories we have seen, Abolition Human Abortion lets savable babies die. They will wait until either the nation has repented completely, there is a perfect constitutional petition, or the perfect laws are passed.

2. The Local Church? AHA's Bride Without a Body

Martin's warning about theological term switching is definitely in play here. When pressed about local church attendance, AHA adherents claim to be part of the bride of Christ. However, the bride of Christ has a body. This body is the *church*. Local churches throughout the world make up the "visible" body of Christ. AHA has a twisted view of the church. Anyone who interacts with AHA and its advocates quickly finds conversations going something like this.

119

Bob the Pro-Life Guy: I like your sign, man, By the way, I'm a member of First Baptist Church. Where are you a member?

Al the Abolitionist: I am a part of the bride of Christ. A church is more than a building.

Bob the Pro-Life Guy: Right, but where do you go to church?

Al the Abolitionist: I fellowship with brothers and sisters every Sunday.

Bob the Pro-Life Guy: Right, where?

Al the Abolitionist: My house.

Bob the Pro-Life Guy: Oh, so it's a home church?

Al the Abolitionist: No, it's a home fellowship. There is no local church in the Bible. You can't join a thing that doesn't exist. Anyway, you need to repent for not being an abolitionist. If your church is a 501c3 your pastor is demonic.

Bob the Pro-Life Guy: Um, okay, man.

Al the Abolitionist: No, it's not okay. Babies are dying. Have you read Amos 5 and Isaiah 1?

(Bob the Pro-Life Guy slowly backs away...)

This might seem like an exaggeration, but it really isn't.

In theological terms, the "universal church" is made up of all who have been born again and trusted in Christ as Savior and Lord. AHA is fond of the term "Bride of Christ" as a reference for their view of the universal church. The "Bride of Christ" terminology is found in Revelation 21-22 when John describes the New Jerusalem.

All who trust in Christ by faith are justified and made right with God through the shed blood of Jesus. They are no longer guilty. There is no more condemnation for

121

anyone in this category (Rom. 8:1.) Anyone who is born again is going to heaven because they are justified by faith (Rom. 5:1-2). Jesus calls everyone to be born again (Jn. 3:3). Christians who get saved on their deathbeds are not able to join a local church, but they are all in heaven now. The thief on the cross is in heaven and was not able to join a local church (Matthew 26).

So far, so good. I doubt anyone from AHA would disagree with this. If John gets saved Thursday night, and is hit by a bus Friday morning. He is in heaven forever. He has been justified by faith.

But there is such a thing as a *local or specific church.* The Greek word for church is *ekklesia.* It appears 34 times in the New Testament and each time it literally means a specific place, where believers are "called out" from the world into a specific location. There are specific churches where believers were addressed in the New

Testament, such as the church at Rome and Thessalonica.

These churches were given instructions on how to govern

themselves with elders and deacons in Titus and Timothy.

Membership of local members of local churches is

mentioned in Hebrews 13 and Matthew 18 by Jesus

Himself. Offices in the church are given by St Paul in

Ephesians 4.

Now, in the 21st century not every church is

preaching the gospel. Many mainline denominations in the

United States are sadly compromised. Some even support

abortion. But to deny that local churches are biblical or

necessary because Christians are automatic members of the

"helpmate bride of Christ" is absurd and biblically

inconsistent. It reveals Abolish Human Abortion's
theological confusion with justification and the gifts of the

Spirit.

Many AHA members claim to fellowship like Al the Abolitionist does above, but are home churches really necessary in the 21st century? Of course, there were churches that met in homes during New Testament times like the one mentioned in the book of Philemon. But more often than not, when the church is not facing open persecution, or if you don't live in the middle of North Dakota or something, it should not be too difficult for an abolitionist to find a church and become a member as Christ taught. Otherwise you are in an echo chamber with friends who are too self-righteous or proud to submit to others. This root of individualism leads to, yet again, the bad fruits we see in Abolish Human Abortion.

The bottom line is this: If you believe that you are too theologically astute, or too much of an abolitionist to join a local church, then you are proud and need to repent.

The church is not about you. It's about the gospel. It's

about Jesus. And, wouldn't it make sense to spread the

principles of abolitionism around to the evangelical

churches? Otherwise, AHA doctrine will remain isolated.

As Martin said, "It is simple for a cultist to *spiritualize*

and *redefine* the clear meaning of Biblical text and

teachings so as to be in apparent harmony with the historic

Christian faith. However, such a harmony is based upon

double earnings of words which cannot stand the test of

Biblical context, grammar, or sound exegesis. [20]

Part of the problem seems to be Abolish Human

Abortion's confusion between justification and

sanctification. As Martin says, "To spiritualize texts and
doctrines, or attempt to explain them away on the basis of

---

[20] Ibid, p. 21

the nebulous phrase, "interpretation," is scholastic dishonesty, and it is not uncommonly found in leading cult literature." [21]When AHA claims that Abolish Human Abortion is "not a group, but a symbol or an ideology," they are muddying the waters of definitions. They are committing scholastic dishonesty. Martin continues, "On encountering a cultist then, always remember that you are dealing with a person who is familiar with Christian terminology., and who has carefully redefined it to fit the system of thought he or she now embraces."[22] AHA

definitely shows some qualities of cultishness, if not outright cultishness.

Martin says the following about encountering a cultist.

---

[21] Ibid, p. 22
[22] Ibid, p. 20

"The belief systems of the cults are characterized by closed-mindedness. They are not interested in a rational cognitive evaluation of the facts. The organizational structure interprets the facts to the cultist, generally invoking the Bible and/or their respective founders [--such as Wilberforce or Garrison, emphasis mine--] as the ultimate source of their pronouncements. Such belief systems are in isolation, they never shift to logical consistency. They exist in what we might describe as separate compartments in the cultist's mind and are almost incapable of penetration or disruption if the individual cultist is completely committed to the pattern of his organization." [23]

Let me be clear here. There is an odd uniformity to AHA adherents that is troubling. They seem to have

---

[23] Ibid, p. 24

memorized the same type of doctrine (all the while claiming it is not a doctrine) and ask the same types of questions and offer the same type of answers and justifications. While I am not calling them a cult, I am saying that their acolytes often sound like brainwashed cult members. And this is exactly what the pro-life movement does not need.

"Secondly, cultic belief systems are characterized by genuine antagonism on a personal level since the cultist almost always his portrays his dislike of the Christian message with the messenger who holds such opposing beliefs."[24]

If your movement has begun by insulting the people that you say you want to talk to, if your movement is known for soaring incendiary rhetoric, such as calling pro-life

---

[24] Ibid, p. 25

Christians to repent of their inauguration of Satan, you are setting yourself up for isolation. In fact, this might even be part of the plan all along. You believe the church is compromised. So you do some kind of gotcha video of the church leaders asking you to take the signs down. Then you parade around the internet like you are a martyr for the cause, when all you have really done is made an unwarranted assumption about fellow believers in Christ. You start lying about their motives. You assume the church doesn't want to talk to you, you act as offensive as possible, and then when you are removed from the premises while imagining yourself as the next Apostle Paul.

This behavior helps no one. It's not saving any babies. It's offensive to all involved, especially to God whose body you are abusing. Jesus doesn't treat His bride this way. Put the cameras away and go to church. Serve your brothers and sisters instead of self-righteously condemning them. Be planted in fertile soil (a local church) where good strong roots can lead to Christ-like "fruits".

Martin continues:
"Since almost all systems of authority in cult organizations indoctrinate their disciples to believe that anyone who opposes their beliefs cannot be motivated by anything other than satanic force or blind prejudice and ignorance, a cultist's encounter with Christians who do not fit this pattern can produce startling results." [25]

If AHA really believes that a vast majority of pro-lifers have inaugurated Satan, then this sentence from Martin makes sense. We aren't on the same side apparently. However, if referencing Moloch and Satan is just a way to get attention and if AHA is embarrassed by these phrases as a youthful indiscretion, then maybe we can

---

[25] Ibid, p. 25

work together. We all say passionate things we don't really mean in the heat of battle. As of this writing, it does not seem that way.

Further, Martin says, "Above all else Christians must learn that most cults consider that they have freed their adherents from religious exploitation which they almost always accuse historic Christianity of practicing." [26]

See, they are not "pro-life" they are abolitionists. As Martin wrote, they are "freeing" their adherents in this way. The term "pro-life" is not biblical. The term "pro-life" is exploitative, etc.

Martin continues, "Thirdly, almost without exception cultic belief systems all manifest a type of institutional dogmatism and a pronounced intolerance for any position but their own. This no doubt stems from the

---

[26] Ibid, p. 25

fact that in the case of non-Christian cult systems which wish

to be identified with Christianity the ground for their claims

is almost always supernatural." [27]

The leaders of Abolish Human Abortion were

disciplined and removed from their church fellowship in

2012. Trinity Baptist Church of Norman, OK, a

conservative-Bible-believing pro-life fellowship was

originally involved with AHA. As their pastor Ronny put to

me, they are "pro-life in every way."

However, the leaders of AHA specifically had their

philosophy and agenda. They were unwilling to yield to the

elders of the church and the Scriptures. Despite the New

Testament's call to unity in Titus 3:10, Romans 16:17-18,

and 1 Cor. 1:10-13, the leaders of AHA, some of whom

grew up in the church, left to start their own fellowship of

---

[27] Ibid, p. 26

believers rather than sit under the leadership of Trinity

Baptist Church. All because Trinity Baptist Church did not

support their approach and beliefs about how to be pro-

life—or better than pro-life—to be an abolitionist!

The isolationism of AHA is toxic to the unity of the

broader movement. AHA needs to repent.

Is AHA a cult? No. They believe all the traditional

doctrines of the Christian faith. However, they are close.

Their confusion on the doctrine of justification and their

hostile rejection of the local church as opposed to the

universal church causes problems for their adherents and

for others in the pro-life movement. They need to repent

and change. My prayer for AHA is for these sincere

brothers to join local churches, to work with already existing

pro-life ministries, and to repent of their pride. If they do

so, they will be blessed beyond measure, and the battle

133

against abortion will gain a powerful and passionate ally.

CHAPTER SEVEN:
PRINCIPLES AND METHODS—IMMEDIATISM and INCREMENTALISM

The best way to describe AHA's definitions of

incrementalism and immedatism is by showing absurd

examples. Their distinctions are illogical and biblically

inconsistent.

Imagine you are on a baseball team. Your team is

losing 3-0 in the bottom of the ninth inning. Three more

outs and the game is over. What does your team need?

Well, you need runs, hits, baserunners, and probably a little

bit of luck. In other words, you're desperate. Or you're just

a Mariners fan and you're used to it. Either way, these are

the things you need. These are the pragmatic steps you

need to take to meet your ideal goal.

There are several ways you can get on base. You can

135

get a hit. You can walk. You can get hit by a pitch. You can run on a dropped third strike. Now, is it wrong to get to first base? No. Is it wrong to hit a solo homerun? Is it wrong to walk? Is it wrong to hit a single? Of course not. So, let's assume you hit a solo homerun. If the score is 3 to 1 after your homerun, are your teammates going to criticize you for not hitting a grand slam? Of course not. Why? There were no teammates on base, and the bases weren't loaded which means a grand slam *was not even a possibility.* The most you could do was hit a solo home run. You did the absolute best you could given the circumstances.

This illustrates the problem that Abolish Human Abortion has with the distinctions between immediatism and incrementalism. AHA claims to be immediatists, which means they are calling for an immediate end to abortion, now. This is a good thing. So is every other pro-lifer in this fight. However, they incorrectly claim that incrementalism (which describes everyone else except the organization-non-organization) is an actual deal with the devil, or Moloch or whoever.

But here we see a categorical mistake of the highest order. In philosophy, a category mistake is made when definitions are confused either intentionally or accidentally. It is a logical fallacy.

Imagine visiting the University of Miami. You walk around the campus and see the beautiful buildings and palm trees. You turn to a student walking past you and ask, "Excuse me, where is the University of Miami?"

The student is puzzled. "It's here," she says.

You continue. "But where?

Her puzzlement abides. "It's *here*. You *are at* the University of Miami." It's *these* buildings, *that* parking

137

garage, and *those* dorms over there."

Obviously, there is no building or place that contains the entire university, so the category mistake is made. You're here already.

How does this relate to incrementalism and immediatism?

Abolish Human Abortion's representatives commit a category mistake by emphasizing immediatism instead of incrementalism. Often in discussions, AHA adherents will ask a pro-lifer, "Are you an incrementalist or an immediatist?" But this question is similar to the confusion above with our visitor from the University of Miami. For AHA, everyone who is part of their organization-non-organization is an incrementalist. *Immediatists* refuse to compromise and demands that abortion be outlawed now. On the other side are incrementalists. *Incrementalists* are compromisers, pure and simple. In fact, incrementalists probably don't even want abortion to be outlawed. This is the tone one gets from Abolish Human Abortion. This is a startling example of their bad roots are corrupting their tone with others. Their imbalance and confusion are leading to bad fruit.

But it isn't that easy. Of course, Christians are not to compromise the truths of the Scripture in their personal lives. It would be foolish indeed for a Christian man to think that it is a good compromise to look at pornography one day a week instead of seven days a week. He should get rid of it completely. In our individual lives, we should live uncompromised lives as we pursue holiness unto the Lord (Heb. 12:14). We should turn from sin immediately and repent in our lives by the saving grace of the Lord Jesus Christ and the Holy Spirit who indwells within.

139

However, when it comes to abortion, we live in a pluralistic society where there are countless views and opinions. It is not just up to us. Not only is our nation divided politically, but it is divided among Christians and non-Christians. 120 million Americans voted in the last Presidential election. It is hard to build consensus on many issues, especially the issue of abortion. Immediatism is not a wise philosophy to move any social issue forward, especially in a pluralistic and relativistic country of almost 320 million people. Is this an accurate representation of America? Yes.

Most states cannot get an abortion ban through their respective legislatures. What should be done then? How you answer this question determines a lot about whether you are an immediatist or an incrementalist. The pro-life movement has responded by submitting ultrasound bills, parental notification bills, 20-week bans, fetal pain bills, heartbeat bills, defunding abortion services through Medicaid, and basically any legislation they can get passed *in order to save as many babies as possible.* And these bills have largely accomplished these goals. These incremental pragmatic steps are moving the pro-life movement towards its ideological goal. It's not a grand slam. But it is a win.

But AHA criticizes these bans as attempts to compromise the truth of the gospel. Again, they seem to forget that compromise in a *believer's life* is one thing but compromising in politics to get the most and best pro-life legislation passed is quite another. To use our baseball analogy, AHA criticizes the player for not hitting a grand slam when all he could possibly do was hit a solo homerun. Acolytes of Abolish Human Abortion apparently prefer that since a grand slam is impossible, no one should even step up to the plate.

The organization that is not an organization, AHA, remains on the sidelines, criticizing and hindering laws that have helped save babies, while lionizing their impossible dreams of a total abortion ban as the only way to live life "in a culture that practices child sacrifice." But it is not uncompromising holiness, it's misguided retreatism. Ideas have consequences. This rotting fruit is the result of some bad roots.

We can do better. Bad fruit cannot be cut off and replaced with good fruit until the entire root is torn up and replanted with a healthier root. Abolish Human Abortion needs to admit that incremental bills have saved lives. AHA representatives need to learn to work with those who have submitted and written these bills. They need to see every life saved as a victory. They need to tear up their bad roots, build their foundation on consistent biblical teaching, join in the efforts of faithful pro-lifers, and repent of their divisive

methods. We are one body in Christ. We need to stop

attacking ourselves.

When they do so, they will be part of the solution

for the disunity that plagues the pro-life movement.

CHAPTER EIGHT:

A GOOD TESTIMONY WITH THOSE OUTSIDE?

The aged prophet stood before the crowd. He knew he was about to die. He had been faithful to His calling, His people, and His God. But he wasn't done. He had something to ask the people.

"Then Samuel said to all Israel, "Behold, I have listened to your voice in all that you said to me and I have appointed a king over you. "Now, here is the king walking before you, but I am old and gray, and behold my sons are with you. And I have walked before you from my youth even to this day. "Here I am; bear witness against me before the LORD and His anointed. Whose ox have I taken, or whose donkey have I taken, or whom have I defrauded? Whom have I oppressed, or from whose hand have I taken a bribe to blind my eyes with it? I will restore *it* to

you." They said, "You have not defrauded us or oppressed

us or taken anything from any man's hand." He said to

them, "The LORD is witness against you, and His anointed

is witness this day that you have found nothing in my hand."

And they said, "*He is* witness." (1 Sam. 12:1-6)

Similarly, the Apostle Paul tells us, "My conscience

is clear but that does not make me innocent." (1 Cor. 4:4)

When you are part of a pro-life ministry, or any

ministry for that matter, it is essential not just *what* your

ministry does, but *how* it is done as well. Obviously, we

must be true to God's word. But we also should do right by

those who are watching, both in the world and in the

church. Methods matter.

This is doubly important for a pro-life ministry.

Remember, one out of every four women in the United

States have had at least one abortion. We must realize we are interacting with millions of post abortive women and men. We must make sure we are not just *doing the right things but doing them the right way.* We must have biblically consistent methods. Fortunately, we have many to choose from.

Consider Paul's instructions for church leadership in the New Testament.

"This *is* a faithful saying: If a man desires the position of a bishop,[a] he desires a good work. [2] A bishop then must be blameless, the husband of one wife, temperate, sober-minded, of good behavior, hospitable, able to teach; [3] not given to wine, not violent, not greedy for money,[b] but gentle, not quarrelsome, not covetous; [4] one who rules his own house well, having *his* children in submission with all reverence [5] (for if a man does not know how to rule his own house, how will he take care of the church of God?); [6] not a novice, lest being puffed up with pride he fall into the *same* condemnation as the devil. [7] Moreover he must have a good testimony among those who are outside, lest he fall into reproach and the snare of the devil." (1 Tim. 3:1-7)

These are the standards given for leading a ministry of any kind. Humility. We must be humble. We must manage our houses well. Effective leadership. We must be gentle and kind. Peaceable. However, note the final admonition in these verses above. Reputation. We must have a good testimony with those who are "outside". We can't just "not care" what people think. The world is watching. If we don't care about what people outside are thinking, the devil is waiting with snares to capture us. This is serious. Without the proper roots, unbiblical fruits will abound.

147

Further, in Titus 3, Paul says, "Remind them to be subject to rulers and authorities, to obey, to be ready for every good work, [2] to speak evil of no one, to be peaceable, gentle, showing all humility to all men. [3] For we ourselves were also once foolish, disobedient, deceived, serving various lusts and pleasures, living in malice and envy, hateful and hating one another. [4] But when the kindness and

the love of God our Savior toward man appeared, [5] not by works of righteousness which we have done, but according to His mercy He saved us, through the washing of regeneration and renewing of the Holy Spirit, [6] whom He poured out on us abundantly through Jesus Christ our Savior, [7] that having been justified by His grace we should become heirs according to the hope of eternal life. [8] This is a

faithful saying, and these things I want you to affirm constantly, that those who have believed in God should be careful to maintain good works. These things are good and profitable to men. [9] But avoid foolish disputes, genealogies, contentions, and strivings about the law; for they are unprofitable and useless. [10] *Reject a divisive man after the first and second admonition,* [11] knowing that such a person is warped and sinning, being self-condemned. (Titus 3:1-11)

And in Ephesians, he writes, "I, therefore, the prisoner of the Lord, beseech you to walk worthy of the calling with which you were called, [2] with all lowliness and gentleness, with longsuffering, bearing with one another in love,[3] endeavoring to keep the unity of the Spirit in the bond of peace.[4] *There is* one body and one Spirit, just as you were called in one hope of your calling; [5] one Lord, one faith, one baptism; [6] one God and Father of all, who *is* above all, and through all, and in you[a] all." (Eph 4:1-6)

Further in Ephesians 4, Paul exhorts us. "Let no corrupt word proceed out of your mouth, but what is good for necessary edification, that it may impart grace to the hearers." (Eph. 4:29) Only a few verses later, he tells us to expose the deeds of unrighteousness, (Eph. 5:11) which

149

happens to be AHA's favorite verse. However, these verses

only make sense in the context of the local church, not the

sins of the people at large.

Finally, in his instructions to the church at Philippi,

Paul writes:

"Therefore, my beloved and longed-for

brethren, my joy and crown, so stand fast in the Lord,

beloved.[2] I implore Euodia and I implore Syntyche to be of

the same mind in the Lord. [3] And[a] I urge you also, true

companion, help these women who labored with me in the

gospel, with Clement also, and the rest of my fellow

workers, whose names *are* in the Book of Life. [4] Rejoice in

the Lord always. Again I will say, rejoice! [5] Let your

gentleness be known to all men. The Lord *is* at hand.[6] Be

anxious for nothing, but in everything by prayer and

supplication, with thanksgiving, let your requests be made

known to God; [7] and the peace of God, which surpasses all understanding, will guard your hearts and minds through Christ Jesus." (Phil. 4:1-7)

Our gentleness must be evident to all. Not our signs. Not our anger. Not our unresolved bitternesses. Not our daddy issues. Our gentleness. Were there atrocities and injustice occurring in the Roman empire while Paul wrote the book of Philippians? Absolutely. But what did Paul emphasize? Principled compassion. Service to the body of Christ by joining in membership and accountability with them. Gentleness and joyfulness. For the fruit of the Spirit is joy. The fruit of the Spirit is kindness. The fruit of the Spirit is peace.

May it be true of us all, by God's grace.

CHAPTER NINE:

A TEST CASE: THE BOTCHED CAMPAIGN OF DAN FISHER FOR OKLAHOMA GOVERNOR

Oklahoma is one of the most conservative, pro-life states in our land. Only two abortion clinics remain there[28]. To put this in perspective, the population of Oklahoma is almost four million. There are two abortion clinics. Only one clinic for every two million people. In contrast, the population of Florida is almost 20 million. There are 57 clinics in Florida, one for every 350,000 residents. As you can see, Oklahoma is a very conservative, anti-abortion state.

In 2018, Abolish Human Abortion had an incredible opportunity to demonstrate to the nation that they could make Oklahoma the first state to become

---

[28] http://abortiondocs.org/search-results/34/?clinic_type=1&search&state

abortion-free. As a resident of Florida, I would love to have the Sooner State's statistics and demographics. Many in the pro-life community turned their eyes to the Oklahoma gubernatorial campaign.

T. Russell Hunter and other abolitionists became involved in the campaign of former Pastor and State Senator Dan Fisher. Fisher ran as a Republican in crowded field. Hunter, one of the founders of AHA, began working as his communications director. As one can imagine, the polemical and prophetic pronouncements of Hunter made news in a difficult primary campaign. And not the good kind.

Hunter made headlines for claiming publicly that it "would be a sin for anyone to vote against Dan Fisher." When this claim was circulated, the long shot Dan Fisher campaign was basically doomed. Hunter attempted to qualify but did not back down from his statement. [29]In doing

so, he helped to sink the campaign of Fisher. Immediatism

failed.

Additional damage occurred when Hunter was

found impersonating Fisher in a text message with Phoenix

pastor Jeff Durbin. Hunter used his position as Head of

Communications to pose as Dan Fisher in at least one

group of exchanges with Durbin regarding a fundraiser.

This of course was found out, as most lies tend to be. [30]

Methods matter. Maturity matters.

Fisher got eight percent of the vote in one of the

most conservative pro-life states in the nation. The

campaign became about his ineptitude in surrounding

---

[29] (http://www.soonerpolitics.org/editorial/campaign-worker-declares-it-a-sin-to-not-vote-for-dan-fisher)

[30] http://algerhart.blogspot.com/2018/01/dan-fisher-busted.htm

himself with people like Hunter who has no political experience and little social skills. One wonders how it went for Hunter, who spends much of his time insulting and alienating Christians in Oklahoma for a living, when he then had to ask these same folks to consider supporting the AHA candidate for Governor. From the looks of it, it did not go well. The bad fruit that Hunter has been growing precede him.

Recently (late 2018) Hunter and others seem to be continuing their attempts at political inroads throughout the nation by launching another new website. [31] Abolish Human Abortion tried their hand at politics in 2018. Let's hope they never do it again for the sake of the broader movement. At least until they can grow and mature.

---

[31] Freethestates.org

CHAPTER TEN:

TOWARD A THEOLOGY OF PRO-LIFE MISSIONS

Is fighting abortion the church's job?

Of course not.

And of course.

These statements need to be qualified here, so let me unpack this a bit.

In Matthew 28:18-20, Jesus gave the great commission to His apostles. Churches began popping up all over the Mediterranean. They were preaching the gospel, adding to their numbers, lovingly discipling and disciplining their members, and equipping the saints that had been called out of the world. So, where does fighting injustice come in?

The gospel informs our agendas. We have been rescued. We love because He first loved us (1 Jn. 4:19). We

157

were dead in our sins before God gave us life (Eph. 2:1-2). Therefore, we seek to rescue the perishing as we are commanded in Proverbs 24:11-12 and Proverbs 31:8. Defending the helpless should be the natural progression of the gospel's work in our lives.

Practically, pro-life ministry must be connected to the local church for oversight, accountability, and growth. You must be accountable to a body of elders (Heb. 13) *If you will not submit to the Bible's teaching on the local church, then you have no right to expect others to listen to your teaching on abortion.* If your church does not have a pro-life ministry, then pray about how you can begin one, or network with existing ministries in your area. Most abortion clinics are in urban areas, and so if you attend church in a small country town, the abortion issue may not be in the forefront of folks' minds. However, the chances are better that your church would be open to pro-life outreach in a smaller town because most churches in small towns are conservative and more openly pro-life.

FLORIDA: A CASE STUDY

I will conclude with some personal examples. Florida has 57 abortion clinics. However, only 15% of the counties in Florida have an abortion clinic. The northern panhandle of the state has clinics in Pensacola (one), Tallahassee (one), and Jacksonville (four). Only six clinics reside on the 357 mile stretch of interstate 10, and the central and coastal counties before you reach Gainesville (about 50 miles south of I-10) are all abortion free.

So, what's the point of this geography lesson? The counties and cities in these areas are very conservative and pro-life, and this is true in most rural areas across the country. Interested pro-lifers who want to make a difference but who do not live in these areas should network with the groups that are already doing ministry. What can you do? Unite. Maybe take a Saturday and get a group together to do ministry at an abortion clinic that is a few hours away. Take the youth group or the singles ministry. This is a great way to involve the greater body of Christ on the abortion issue.

Many of these counties and rural areas will already have crisis pregnancy centers , churches, or conservative, pro-life political action committees. There will also be Catholic churches in these areas that may already have life ministries in place. Sign up for, or start chapters of awareness campaigns like 40 Days for Life, Walk for Life, March for Life, etc.

The evangelical church in America needs to see that

abortion is more than a political issue. The church needs

activists to help. Here is a brief list of groups that can help

get the small, rural church involved in on site clinic ministry.

40 Days for Life

Pro Life Action Ministries

Florida Preborn Rescue

Cities for Life

End Abortion Now

Life Chain

Sidewalk Advocates for Life

National Right to Life

If the cities and counties without clinics sent

missionaries to the cities that do have clinics, we would have

a huge increase in the amount of on-site activism at the

abortion clinics across the country. By working together, we can do it. Let us work from solid foundational roots of the gospel, unity, humility and accountability. Let us bear fruits of peace. Let us be agents of change and unity, not division. Let us be like Paul who preached faithfully in a pagan and decadent world. Let us shine the light of the gospel into the darkest places in our land.

CONCLUSIONS

We've reached the end. I commend you for reading and finishing this small book. For those of you who are a part of AHA and feel like you are not able to leave, I am praying for you. If you need help, you can contact me personally through my website or my social media sites. You aren't alone. God does not want you to feel trapped somewhere you do not belong. You belong in a local church with elders and biblical leadership. Read and study the Bible. The Bible is not an activist manual for pro-life agitators. It is the story of God coming to His people and saving them for His glory forever. Read the Old and New Testaments. When you do, you will find that the Bible has much to say about the manner in which we minister. God cares deeply about how we reflect His image, His grace, and compassion.

If you have read this book and are in agreement still with the tenets of AHA, I thank you for reading. If you think I have reached these conclusions erroneously, I humbly ask that you reach out to me and let me know where I have erred. If you'd like to debate these things publicly, I would be happy to do that too. May God bless you all and keep you, may He make His face shine down upon you, and give you peace.

Scott J Mahurin, December 4, 2018

BIBLIOGRAPHY

Ertelt, Steven. "David Daledein Vindicated as Judge Dismissed Charges Against Him For Exposing Planned Parenthood." LifeNews.com, 16 June 2016.

Hagelin, Rebecca. "New Study Shows Pro-Life Laws Save Lives." *The Heritage Foundation*,

www.heritage.org/marriage-and-family/commentary/new-study-shows-pro-life-laws-save-lives.

Hays, Steve, et al. Abolition of Reason: Pro-Life Apologists Deconstruct "Immediatist" Ideology as Presented in Cunningham-Hunter Debate. JillStanek.com, 2015, www.jillstanek.com/wp/wp-content/uploads/2015/06/Debate-e-book-small.pdf

Jacoby, Jeff. "American Millennials Rethink Abortion, for Good Reasons - The Boston Globe."*BostonGlobe.com*, 9 June 2015.

Martin, Walter R. The Kingdom of the Cults. Bethany Fellowship, Inc. Publishers. Minneapolis, MN, 1965.

Liptak, Adam. "Supreme Court Strikes Down Texas Abortion Restrictions." *The New York Times,* 27 June 2016.

Roden, G.J. "Unborn Children as Constitutional Persons." *Issues in Law and Medicine.,* U.S. National Library of Medicine, 2010.

Rohrer, Gary. "Federal Judge Blocks New Florida Abortion Law." *OrlandoSentinel.com*, 1 July 2016.

Trewhella, Matthew J. The Doctrine of the Lesser Magistrates: a Proper Resistance to Tyranny and a Repudiation of Unlimited Obedience to Civil Government. Create Space, 2013.

Yonke, Matt. "Voice of Choice Website Removes "Bully List"

Targeting Pro-Life Activists With Harassment." LifeNews.com, 24 Oct. 2014, www.life.news.com/2014/10/23/voice-of-choice-website-removes-bully-list-targeting-pro-life-activists-with-harassment.

ABOUT THE AUTHOR

SCOTT J. MAHURIN is the Founder and Director of Florida Preborn Rescue, a pro-life, non-profit organization based in St. Petersburg, Florida. Founded in 2012, Mr. Mahurin has taught sidewalk counseling and practical ministry at local abortion clinics. He earned B.S. degrees from the University of Idaho in History and Philosophy in 1999. Mr. Mahurin also taught in classical Christian schools for 18 years. He lives in St. Petersburg, Florida, with his wife Rebecca and his three daughters.

54649919R00105

Made in the USA
Columbia, SC
03 April 2019